THE
REALSIMPLE
METHOD TO
ORGANIZING
EVERY ROOM

THE
REALSIMPLE
METHOD TO
ORGANIZING
EVERY ROOM
AND HOW TO KEEP IT THAT WAY

The Editors of Real Simple

©2018 Time Inc. Books, a division of
Meredith Corporation

Published by Oxmoor House,
an imprint of Time Inc. Books
225 Liberty Street, New York, NY 10281

Writer: Julie Vadnal
Senior Editor: Betty Wong
Editorial Assistants: Lauren Moriarty,
    Claire Nist
Project Editor: Lacie Pinyan
Design Director: Melissa Clark
Photo Director: Paden Reich
Designer: Matt Ryan
Assistant Production Manager:
    Diane Rose Keener
Associate Project Manager: Hillary Leary
Copy Editors: Donna Baldone,
    Adrienne Davis

Proofreader: Julie Gillis
Indexer: Mary Ann Laurens
Fellow: Holly Ravazzolo
Cover photograph: Johnny Miller
    Styling: Sarah Smart

For additional credits, see page 267.

ISBN-13: 978-0-8487-5677-2

Library of Congress Control
Number: 2018941155

First Edition 2018

Printed in the United States of America

10 9 8 7 6 5 4 3 2 1

We welcome your comments
and suggestions about Time Inc. Books.
Time Inc. Books
Attention: Book Editors
P.O. Box 62310
Tampa, Florida 33662-2310

Time Inc. Books products may be purchased
for business or promotional use. For
information on bulk purchases, please
contact Christi Crowley in the Special Sales
Department at (845) 895-9858.

Contents

6 Preface

8 Introduction: Get Organized, Stay Organized

12 How to Decide What Should Stay and What Should Go

16 Get the Family Involved

18
CHAPTER 1
The Entryway

36
CHAPTER 2
The Living Room

66
CHAPTER 3
The Kitchen

92
CHAPTER 4
The Dining Room

114
CHAPTER 5
The Bedroom

140
CHAPTER 6
The Bathroom

164
CHAPTER 7
The Home Office

194
CHAPTER 8
The Laundry Room

214
CHAPTER 9
The Kids' Bedroom

234
CHAPTER 10
The Outdoor Spaces

264 Our Experts

264 Resources

266 Credits

268 Index

You probably have a space in your home where you put the things you don't know what to do with. We all have these orphan items that find a temporary home in a drawer, a nook, a shelf, or perhaps a whole closet or basement wall—and sometimes that space becomes a permanent home. Which is fine, except for the niggling, nagging knowledge in the back of your brain that if you don't assign things a proper place, you won't be able to find them when you need them.

By using *The Real Simple Method to Organizing Every Room*, you can give happy homes to all those orphan items, so you can spend less time hunting for that stray receipt or cord or scarf, and more time doing the things you truly enjoy.

All this is easier when you're in the right mood. Here are a few mantras that *Real Simple* editors have found to help get—and stay—in the organizing frame of mind:

THOU SHALT NOT TRANSFER CLUTTER

Don't bury the dresser top to save the coffee table.

DOUBLES ARE TROUBLE

You don't need two can openers or five tweezers. Toss duplicates.

KEEP IT WHERE YOU USE IT

Stash toner with the printer and the T.P. under the bathroom sink.

MAKE LABELS, NOT WAR

Mark shelves, bins, and boxes so your family (and houseguests) know where everything goes.

HAVE A PLACE FOR NOTHING

Aim to create one empty cabinet, shelf, or drawer in each room. This is your backup spot when the balance tips. (And it will tip.)

PICK YOURSELF UP, DUST YOURSELF OFF, AND START ALL OVER AGAIN

Organizing is a circle, not a straight line.

We hope the Real Simple Method becomes your own method—and results in a calmer, cleaner, and more carefree home for you and your loved ones.

EDITOR-IN-CHIEF, REAL SIMPLE

Get Organized, Stay Organized

Not all of us are natural born organizers, and that's okay. You may have tried other strategies, systems that suggest hiding clutter in storage bins or that recommend ruthlessly cutting back on what you consider "necessities." But there's one point that all organizing methods can pretty much agree on: **having an organized and thoughtfully arranged home is important to our well-being.**

And so the Real Simple Method is just that—an organizing plan with your well-being and self-care in mind. It's all about creating small, simple habits that make a big impact on everyday life. The Real Simple Method is here to help you think of your home in new ways, so that a bedroom chair isn't just a dumping ground for morning outfit rejects—it's a comfy place to settle in at the end of the day or to sip coffee in the morning. We're not asking you to make miracles happen or change your personality overnight (though you might feel like you've accomplished a minor miracle after making some of the changes in this book). Instead, the goal of the Real Simple Method is to set up organizing systems in your home, inspire you with new ideas that fit your lifestyle, and most importantly, help you and your family stick to those systems going forward. And even if you naturally lean more towards an organized lifestyle, the hacks and tricks we recommend might still surprise you. After all, is there such a thing as too organized? We don't think so.

We've divided this book up by rooms, and within each chapter we share with you the items you need (and the ones you don't) for setting up a well-organized home as well as tips and strategies from the best organizers in the business.

This book will help you organize your home, but it will also make you a more organized person. That's because organized people are not only efficient with their space, but with their time. For example, organized people don't spend ten minutes searching for the remote among the couch cushions; they've already got their feet propped up and are halfway through the opening credits. But it's not just missing on out TV marathons

that's at stake here. It's family time, it's self-care time, and it's chill-and-say-"ahhh" time. Taking the time now to arrange your home in an artful way means you'll just have more time to do things that aren't, well, organizing.

The Real Simple Method is about small changes that make a big impact. For starters, you'll **put an organizational system into place.** This is the time when you'll roll up your sleeves, dig in, and attack that garage or front-hall closet. It's when you'll evaluate your space and see if you're really arranging it in a way that reflects how you use it. It's when you'll install new shelving, or rearrange the hangers in your closet so that all your white shirts live together. Putting a new system into place is the biggest step, and it's also the most important, because it dictates how well you'll stick to your new plan. And the good news about this step? You really should only have to do it once.

Once you've set up your new pristine space and cooed over your photo-ready bookshelves, it's time to partake in the next important step of the Real Simple Method: **Do a little bit each day.** Maintaining order at home is not about spending every weekend decluttering the piles that built up throughout the week. Instead, keep your new system in place by putting things back where they belong every day, like making sure your car keys hit the tray when you walk in the door, or that blankets go back to their baskets before you turn in for the night. You'll thank yourself in the morning.

Another easy strategy for keeping down the clutter is one you'll see a lot within the pages of this book: **Stick to a strict "one in, one out" policy.** When a bookshelf is full, give yourself no other option than to donate what doesn't fit. Same with your closet, or the shoe pile by the front door. When something new comes in, something old must go. While this rule may seem harsh (and choosing between your favorite books can sometimes feel like you're choosing between children), you're doing yourself a bigger disservice by letting overflow take over. Besides, books make wonderful gifts.

At this point, if it sounds like we're suggesting that you're the only one creating and keeping up your newly organized home, well, no. Another important part of the Real Simple Method is that you'll **get everyone in the family involved in the organizing process** from the start. After all, the whole family uses the living room, so why shouldn't they have a say in how it's arranged to fit their needs, too? (That being said, you and your partner might want to do the home office or the kitchen tools yourselves.) When everyone is involved from the beginning, they begin to see why order is needed, and they'll be more invested in keeping the front-hall closet, for example, from becoming a black hole. Oftentimes, children crave order and structure—just look at their classrooms, which often have organizing principles in place from preschool on. And when everyone is a part of the plan, that means everyone gets to enjoy downtime that much more.

But the real payoff to implementing the Real Simple Method—setting up a system, doing a little bit each day, and getting the family involved—extends far beyond breathing a sigh of relief when the in-laws drop by unexpectedly or when a neighbor shows up for an impromptu glass of vino. And it's more than just teaching your children habits that they'll (hopefully) bring with them to college and beyond. Getting organized and clearing out physical clutter can lead to less mental clutter. If you're not worried about your messy bed back at home, you can focus on your daily tasks in the office or the side hustle you're launching. And over time, you'll start to realize that the little moves you were making every day—like cleaning off the countertops and arranging the throw pillows—aren't just changing your home. They're changing your entire outlook.

How to Decide What Should Stay and What Should Go

Whether you're editing down your closet or the junk drawer, it's never easy to toss things that you once loved and spent hard-earned cash on. *Real Simple's* three-step process will help you hang on to only the things you need and love. And as for the rejects? We've got the best ways to donate and sell them. Because that pleather skirt from another life may indeed be worth something—to someone else.

Step 1

Prep For the Purge

If you're not careful, a closet or cabinet clean-out can eat up your weekend and take over your whole house. Start with a game plan to keep it contained.

SET A DATE

Ideally, you want to allocate four hours—that's the amount of time stylists and organizers say it takes to overhaul and reassemble the average closet. Besides, most people reach their saturation point after a morning or an afternoon on the job. Can't budget a window of time that big? Tackle categories (for your closet it might be blouses, lingerie, jewelry, etc; or if you're doing the garage, it's tools, gardening, sports equipment, etc.) in one- or two-hour time blocks spread out over a couple of weeks.

GATHER SUPPLIES

To clean out your closet, you'll need a full-length mirror and seamless underwear for try-ons and heavy-duty trash bags for sorting castoffs. For the junk drawer or home office? You just need a big trash bag. (Same for most other spaces.) Use a Sharpie marker and Super Sticky Post-it Notes to label the bags to donate, tailor, and sell—plus recycle, for items too trashed to be wearable.

INVITE A FRIEND (OPTIONAL)

Simulate the client-stylist experience by asking a pal or sibling whose taste and opinion you trust to help "yay" and "nay" items and keep you moving swiftly along. Another fun pal to have along? A glass of wine or fun music can help make the cleanout seem like less of a chore and more of a celebration.

LAY IT ALL OUT

If you've committed to a one-shot clean-out, pull everything out of the space you're organizing and arrange it by category on the floor. Getting a bird's-eye view allows you to spot themes (for example, too many hammers, or 17 pairs of sandals) and get rid of pieces that aren't pulling their weight. If you're going the micro-organizing route, focusing on one category at a time can also be revelatory. ("Why do I have four gray sweaters?") This ensures that your space stays habitable while you chip away at the project.

Step 2

Should it stay, or should it go?

First things first: Don't think—just dump. Power-sort the items that you love or use/wear all the time into a keep pile and the ones that you know aren't working (and aren't worth something) into a donate or recycle bag. After the power sort, you're ready for the elimination round. To determine what to keep or toss, ask yourself the following questions. Answers of "no/meh" and "rarely/never" should lead to the dump pile. For "yes" or mixed responses, continue on to the next question.

Start Here

QUESTION 1: DOES IT SERVE YOU?

This one powerful question can help eliminate the majority of clutter in your life. What the question is really asking is, "Does it make you feel good?" If it's a closet item, do you get compliments when you wear it—or are you always tugging at it uncomfortably?

QUESTION 2: DOES IT GO WITH OTHER ITEMS IN YOUR HOME?

A streamlined home is like a symphony, with pieces that work together harmoniously in many combinations. Instead of assigning items specific roles (these are my fancy candlesticks) and hoarding these things in a drawer, imagine that your home or your closet is a boutique where everything works together.

QUESTION 3: ARE YOU GOING TO ACTUALLY USE IT?

Instead of peering into the past with the old "Have you used it in the last six months?" question, think about the future. Will you really start to make acai seed bowls for breakfast, or should you toss the bag of acai seeds that have been sitting in the pantry for months? Or, for your closet, would you don that strappy dress to work if you had the right cardigan to go with it? Make notes on a shopping list. Let it go if you try to justify keeping it with the idea that you'll use it "maybe someday, when I lose weight/become a person who loves acai bowls."

QUESTION 4: IS IT THE BEST VERSION?

If the style is passé, the fit is unflattering, or you've been keeping it in the kitchen cabinet since Aunt Kathy gifted it to you for your wedding 15 years ago when fondue was actually a thing, it might be time for an upgrade in appliances or fashion.

QUESTION 5: IS IT HIGH-MAINTENANCE?

Does it require refueling or a special cleaner? (Cast iron, we're looking at you.) Or, in your closet, does the effort of handwashing or the expense of dry-cleaning keep you from wearing it? Then it's time to face the facts and sub in something less fussy.

QUESTION 6: DOES IT HAVE SENTIMENTAL VALUE?

You don't have to part with your dad's baseball mitt or a blanket that Grandma knit. Just limit memorabilia to one storage box in a closet. As for the necklace your ex gave you that was never your style—just, why? Resolve to move on. Another option for a memento you just can't part with: Take a photo, then toss the piece.

STILL ON THE FENCE? PARK THE ITEM IN QUESTION IN A PROMINENT SPOT (UP FRONT IN THE CABINET OR CLOSET) AND MARK IT WITH A STICKY NOTE "EXPIRATION DATE" THAT'S TWO MONTHS FROM NOW. IF YOU DON'T REACH FOR THE PIECE WITHIN THAT TIME FRAME, YOU KNOW WHAT TO DO.

Step 3

Optimize your castoffs

Quick! Before you change your mind, round up the rejects and reference the following guides to the best places to donate or sell.

CHARITY CONCERNS

ARE THE DONATION BINS IN PARKING LOTS AND ON STREET CORNERS LEGIT?

You may want to do a little research first. Some of the companies who own them have come under fire for misrepresenting how much of the contributions go to those in need and how much is resold for profit. Goodwill and The Salvation Army are among the most reliable places to unload clothes; some locations pick up for free.

WHAT SHOULD YOU DO WITH THE HOLEY SWEATS THAT YOU THINK NO ONE WANTS?

Donate those, too. Do the sorting team a favor and label bags of beat-up items "recycle." Articles unsuitable for resale in the organizations' stores are sold to textile recyclers, who use the fibers for insulation, carpet padding, and stuffing for toys.

WHERE TO DONATE

Goodwill and The Salvation Army are always great choices for dropping off furniture, books, housewares, kitchenware, tools, and other items. But there are other options out there where you can do some good while cleaning out your closet.

TYPES OF ITEMS	WHERE TO DONATE
CLOTHES IN USED CONDITION	Stores such as H&M, Ann Taylor, Loft, Levi's, and The North Face allow shoppers to send or bring in clothing, shoes, and accessories (any brand) in exchange for discounts on purchases. The donated items are then reused or recycled.
OUTDATED DENIM	The Blue Jeans Go Green program (bluejeansgogreen.com) organizes denim drives with universities and retailers. Some of the old jeans will be reborn as insulation for communities in need. Donators receive a discount to buy a new pair.
WELL-WORN SNEAKERS	Thanks to the Nike Reuse-A-Shoe program, you can bring up to 10 pairs (any label) to a Nike or Converse retail store or mail them to the recycling facility. There the rubber, foam, and fabric from the shoes are ground into a material used to make sports and playground surfaces and new Nike products.
FORMAL WEAR	BridesAcrossAmerica.com puts wedding gowns into the hands of military brides. As for other fancy frocks, direct them to Project G.L.A.M. (wgirls.org), which distributes prom dresses to needy high schoolers.
OLD EYEGLASSES	Send used specs to New Eyes for the Needy (new-eyes.org) and they will be dispensed to adults and children in developing nations or recycled to raise funds for new eyeglasses for disadvantaged Americans.
BOOKS	Many libraries accept donations year-round; what they don't need for their own stock, they sell at a fundraiser. If your local school or library doesn't accept used books, donate to troops through Operation Paperback or to students through Books for Africa and International Book Project. Pack donations in small boxes (easier to lift when full), and toss anything torn or stained.

Hot trends, designer names, tags still attached. These are a few things that may score you beaucoup bucks—without much effort. Online resale sites vary in terms of the types of items they accept, their commission rates, and the level of DIY involved. Below are vitals on some of the top contenders.

RESALE SITE	WHAT TO SELL	HOW TO SELL	AVERAGE PRICE	YOUR PAYOUT
POSHMARK.COM	Unused makeup, fast fashion, luxury and vintage women's clothing in new or gently used condition. Buyers browse members' "closets" and attend virtual shopping events centered on a designer, a product, or a trend.	Snap photos with your phone and identify one for your "cover shot," write a description, and set a price. Mail items to your buyer with a prepaid U.S. Postal Service (USPS) shipping label; you supply the box.	$30 for a mass-market item; $250 for a designer piece	80% on sales of $15 or more; under $15, the company takes a $2.95 commission
THEREALREAL.COM	Pre-owned luxury goods in excellent condition that pass a brand-specific authentication process; menswear, art, and home decorations, too.	Send your items to the company via a free prepaid FedEx shipping label. Pros photograph, price, and list your merch and mail it to the buyer when it sells.	$300 per item	55% to start; 60% if you reach $1,500 in sales; 70% if you reach $10,000
TRADESY.COM	New and gently worn women's fashions in mass-market to designer categories. The site also has more than 50,000 wedding gowns.	Upload photos and include a description. Choose your price, or let the site suggest one. Mail to the buyer with a free prepaid USPS shipping kit.	$20 for a mass-market item; $300 for a designer piece	91% of the sale in store credit; 88% if you want cash
FACEBOOK MARKETPLACE	Anything from kitchen appliances to furniture to collectibles—all to people in your area	Upload a photo, write a description, and list a price. The delivery is up to you and the buyer.	Depends on what you think is fair	100%, you and the buyer work out the method (cash, Venmo, or Paypal)
CRAIGSLIST.ORG	Everything and the kitchen sink. The site is a good place to move your furniture, appliances, or kids' gear.	Highlight the brand and price in your ad title. List dimensions, shape, age, and other important features in the description. Be up front about any flaws, and upload a photo.	Depends on item type and condition; check similar listings before pricing	100%. Postings are free; no commission. Buyers and sellers make delivery arrangements between themselves.

Get the Family Involved

NO, YOU'RE NOT THE ONLY ONE RESPONSIBLE FOR MAKING SURE YOUR HOME IS PILE-FREE. HERE'S HOW TO ROUND UP THE TROOPS AND MAKE SURE EVERYONE'S IN ON THE PLAN.

Tell Them As A Couple (If You're in One)

Announcing a new organizational system or family plan for sorting shoes is more likely to stick if it comes from both parents as a united front. That way, neither one of you will seem like the "good cop, bad cop," and it shows that you're both serious about keeping clutter at bay. (Along these lines, make sure you hold each other accountable to the plan.) And even though you're making the announcement mostly for your kids, a group meeting also helps reinforce the rules for whichever one of you is more prone to slipping up.

Devise a Chore Chart

Keep everyone on track with a chart or make your own. Section out a magnetic dry-erase board by family member, and create one section marked "Chores." Then, use a label maker to mark magnets with different chores, such as "Front door shoe pile" or "Do laundry." Divide up the tasks. When they're done, they can put it back in the chore section. Seeing everything that needs to get done in one place—because kids aren't spending time in the laundry room watching the clothes pile up—is a helpful way for kids to understand the bigger picture of how a household works.

Make Quick Cleanups a Game

Your cell phone timer works wonders. Gather everyone into the living room, set the timer for 5 minutes, and say, "Go!" Suddenly, your everyday tidying is more of a game, and few can argue with such a short timeframe. It especially works for room-to-room cleanups before company is due—you'll be shocked with how much you all can accomplish in just a few minutes.

Give Praise

We won't call it bribing, but there's no harm in saying, "No one can have dessert until we've picked up the toys in the living room." And remember to give praise once a task is done. Your children (and your partner) will feel proud that you've noticed their hard work, and they're more likely to stick to that behavior.

WHAT IF...

Your kids clean up but leave you with streaked mirrors and a jumbled dishwasher—and you're a neat freak.

Wait until the kids are asleep to reload the dishwasher yourself—if you do it in their presence, they might feel like their contributions aren't valued. Going forward, you can teach as you go by saying, "Great, you cleaned the mirror. You know, there's a streak right where my face is. Let's try a paper towel on that."

You stopped fighting your son about keeping his room clean. But now it smells, and there are crusty cereal bowls everywhere.

Before you tell a child that you won't poke your nose in his bedroom, set ground rules. For example: If you're going to eat in your room, bring out the dishes every night or face consequences. Waking him up early to scrub cereal bowls will have an impact as well.

You only want to know the all-age, every-room, no-fail organizing tools you should buy in bulk.

The simple answer: hooks. For coats in the entryway, towels in the bathroom, and jeans you can't get your kid to fold, hooks are the industry-wide solution. Some other ideas? Boat totes. They come in all sizes, they're sturdy, and their role can evolve, from storing toys to carrying laundry. Labels. You can use a Sharpie on washi tape or a label maker. Kids need easy clues about where to put stuff. Trash cans. Place them not just in the kitchen but also by their beds and the couch, too. If kids have to walk across the room to toss a gum wrapper, odds are those wrappers are never going to make it.

You've been doing everything for your kids from Day 1. (Isn't that being a loving mom?) And now they're tweens who don't know where the hamper is.

It's never too late to start teaching them. Sit them down and, in a tone neither mean nor apologetic, say, "You are old enough to help out." If your kids ask why it's so important since you never asked them to help before, add in, "That's our mistake. But you need to learn these things, and it's our job to help you do it."

Chapter 1

The Entryway

SET THE TONE OF YOUR HOME FROM THE MOMENT YOU STEP INSIDE.

CREATING A WARM WELCOME starts in your entryway. It's the first space guests will see when they come over, and it's usually the last place you'll breeze through before running out the door (hopefully, with your car keys this time). So, it's worth making sure your entryway is a pretty and practical space. Artful arranging and sprucing up with fresh flowers and personal objects create an inviting vibe for anyone who passes, whether it's neighbors, in-laws, or, most important, you after a long day.

But a visually pleasing (aka clutter-free) entryway isn't just for when guests are on the itinerary. Being organized as you head out the door in the morning—and knowing exactly where you last set those keys—can make a difference in how you start your day and can also determine how many times you might have to pull back into the driveway to grab something you've forgotten. (It happens.) Plus, having an umbrella or cozy scarf at arm's reach means that you'll be ready when Mother Nature catches you off guard. Finally, trays and tiny baskets create homes for your daily essentials so that you can confidently run out in the morning—and truly unwind from the minute you walk through the door.

If you have the space, set up stations in your mudroom or entryway to help corral clutter. Sports equipment and sunscreen go in cubbies where they're still visible, and all-weather boots stack neatly by the door. (Opposite page) A range of blues—from baby blue paint to a cerulean cushion—makes this functional entryway look clean and cohesive.

THE SECRET TO SETTING A SERENE SCENE FROM THE MOMENT YOU STEP INSIDE IS ALL ABOUT PLACEMENT. BY CREATING A FURNITURE ARRANGEMENT THAT WORKS FOR YOU, MORNINGS WILL BE MADE EASIER, AND YOU'LL BE MORE LIKELY TO KEEP EVERYTHING IN ITS DESIGNATED SPOT.

Follow Your Steps

An efficient way to organize your entryway is to first make sure it's arranged the way you traverse it. If, when you come home, you're crisscrossing the space multiple times on each pass, it's time to reexamine your setup. Think of the order in which you shed your gear (keys, bag, coat, shoes), and move furniture accordingly. If your purse is the first thing you set down, a bench at the doorway might be the perfect place to let it go. Or, if your keys need a home as soon as you breeze through the door, consider a small table with a tray that can be a pretty and practical resting spot.

Set the Table

The best entryway table is slim enough so that it doesn't take up much room—the area is an active thoroughfare, after all—but also wide enough to be utilitarian. Make sure its surface can hold a tray (for mail and keys), a vase, and other decorative objects like picture frames. The table should also be tall enough for baskets to nestle underneath—perfect storage for magazines, books, or umbrellas.

Let Everyone Hang

If you don't have room for a table, a hanging shelf with hooks for keys and other items can do the trick. Does your partner always misplace the dog leash? Your daughter her mittens? Give each member of the family a hook (label them accordingly) by the front door for hanging their essentials. Or, in the springtime, light jackets can find their homes here. (Winter ones are too bulky.) Up top, you'll have room for pretty objects or a notepad for announcements.

A PURPOSELY PETITE DRY-ERASE BOARD ENSURES THAT YOUR PARTING WORDS DON'T GET LOST IN SPACE.

Store Shoes

A tall wicker basket or oversized metal basin can stash shoes vertically—toe-side down, heel-side up, so they're easy to grab and go—and prettily. To prevent overflow, create this house rule: Only one pair per person by the front door. If you're about to add a second pair, the other pair goes to your room. Or, keep footwear clutter down by storing only rain boots by the door. A pair of bright, stylish wellies can even double as décor and rain-shower insurance.

CLEAR OUT THE JUNK— IN FIVE SECONDS

Don't let junk mail get past the foyer. Keep a pretty recycling bag and a shredder by the front door to make daily sorting easy. Many handheld, battery-operated shredders slip discreetly into a drawer.

Start a Returns Bin

A medium-sized basket placed right next to the front door is more than just a drop spot for library books you've read, tools you've borrowed from a neighbor, and clothing purchases you've changed your mind on. It's a visual prompt reminding you to return that stuff (today!).

Go Natural

Fresh flowers can make a big impact and are a nice sight to come home to, even if they last only a week or so. But if you're not the type to commit to new buds every week, go for preserved eucalyptus branches, which are easy to buy online and last forever. They also give off a welcoming, subtle scent.

Prepare for the Elements

Store umbrellas, one for each family member, in a decorative bucket or an extra-large ceramic container near the front door so that they're readily available but not an eyesore. Or, long-handled umbrellas can hang on a coat rack. And why is it that the hardest working shoes (muddy wellies and salty snow boots) are also the toughest to take off? A bench tall enough to tuck galoshes under keeps the action near the door.

Get Reflective

Hanging a mirror on one wall of your entryway can make a small space look bigger and more inviting. Bonus: A mirror by the front door gives you an opportunity to do a "last look" or makeup touch-up before you head out.

"Everything should fit in the space you have allotted for that category of item. Rather than seeing this as a limitation, a mindset shift will allow you to see this as an opportunity to pare down and let go of things you don't really need, wear, or use, and are only holding onto because of a "someday" story or an "it's perfectly good" story. If you don't use it and haven't in at least 12–18 months, someone else would love to, so let it go."

—ANDREW MELLEN, ORGANIZER

Organize This

COVER UP THE <u>COAT CLOSET</u> CHAOS WITH THESE SIMPLE STEPS.

ASSIGN IT OUT

Hang each jacket or coat by family member, then organize from most lightweight to heaviest for each person's coats. To keep it all clear, assign everyone his or her own shade of colored hangers, or tie a piece of colored ribbon to the top of each person's hangers so everyone knows which ones are theirs. (And, so they know where to put them back.)

HANG RIGHT HERE

A hanging organizer can hide small umbrellas, a dog leash, scarves, canvas shopping bags, and keys that you'd prefer hidden from the entryway space.

GO LOW

Store rain and snow boots in a bigger plastic bin, or line the floor with a rubber mat. Look for a mat with a raised rim to keep wet or muddy or snowy footwear from spilling over onto the floor.

KEEP IT CLEAR

Stock the top shelf with a bin to hold adults' hats and gloves, and add one to the floor of the closet for the kiddos. Separating the kids' things from the adults' stuff means you'll never accidentally grab a tiny mitten on your way out to shovel the driveway.

LIGHT IT UP

If your front-hall closet looks like a dark bottomless pit in which to toss all things outerwear, that's exactly how your family will use it? Give this spot a paint job, and install lighting via an LED strip along the underside of the top shelf. It's instantly pretty.

CONTAIN THEIR ENTHUSIASM

When soccer, tennis, or biking (you name it) is in season, catch errant equipment in a low, open-weave metal bin. Implement a weekly search-and-recovery day when everyone is responsible for relocating his or her belongings to their proper places.

The Tools

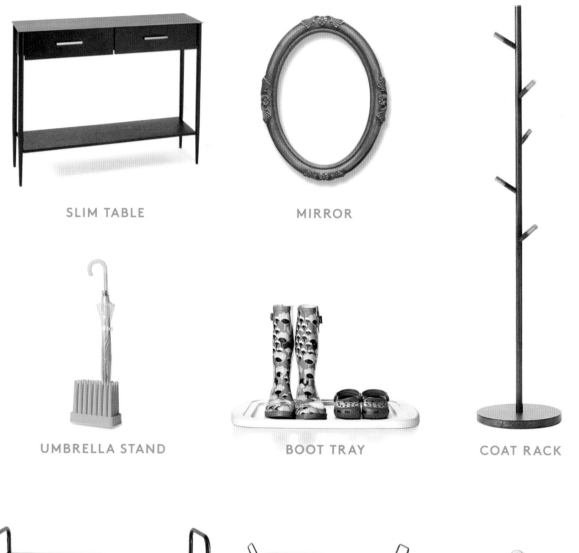

SLIM TABLE

MIRROR

UMBRELLA STAND

BOOT TRAY

COAT RACK

SHOE RACK

METAL OPEN-WEAVE BIN

COLORED HANGERS

ORGANIZING ESSENTIAL

An entryway bench with a shelf for shoes and hidden storage for hats and gloves means that everything will always have its place. It also means you'll have a place to sit while trying to remove a stubborn pair of boots.

WOVEN BASKETS

HOOKS

Whether you are hanging keys or coats, make the most of wall space with a rack or individual hooks and pegs. No room for a table in your entryway? Corral out-the-door items in a wall-mounted mesh basket with key hooks.

DRY-ERASE BOARD

With a mini whiteboard, a patch of wall becomes a place to jot down family notes. Make a stylish dry-erase board using the glass of an old frame with a pretty fabric or paper behind it.

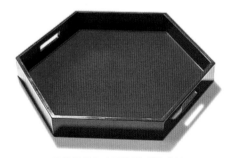

DECORATIVE TRAY

Small-Space Solutions

NOT MANY APARTMENTS ARE DESIGNED WITH A FOYER—SHOCKING, WE KNOW. BUT EVEN IF YOU DON'T HAVE A DEDICATED ENTRYWAY SPACE, YOU STILL NEED A SPOT TO SET YOUR KEYS WHEN YOU WALK IN THE DOOR. TRY THESE TINY-HOME IDEAS.

Float On

Install a narrow, wall-mounted floating shelf next to your door so you have a place to stash your keys and mail as soon as you step inside. Don't have room for a shelf? A picture ledge is even slimmer and can hold envelopes. Add hooks underneath to hang keys, jackets, and bags. Similarly, a mountable magazine rack can hold more than just books and periodicals—tuck light scarves and hats into it, too.

In Fact, Mount Everything

Because you probably don't have room for furniture, wall mount as much as you can—floating dowels to act as hooks, accordion racks to hold practically everything, a mount for your bike, and a mirror, which can also make your space look larger and amplify natural light. Also, a stainless steel kitchen rail, outfitted with S hooks, is a chic way to store shoes without taking up precious floor space.

Use Magnets

Hang magnetic strips or baskets to make the back of your front door (many in apartments are metal) a catchall for mail, keys, notes to remember to pack your lunch, and other small items, like lip balm.

Do Double Duty

A bar cart (or acrylic tray on a stand) can hold your bits and bobs—and your booze. Designate a decorative bowl to corral items that you need on the go, like keys and sunglasses. A midsize woven basket can hide mail until you have time for sorting. Use the rest of the top tray for a hardy potted plant or pretty bottles of the good stuff.

The Real Simple
Method Checklist

IF YOU HAVE . . .

15 Minutes

☐ **HIDE THE BIG STUFF.** Coats, shoes, purses, and packages all need a place to live—stat. Either throw them all in the closet and shut the door (phew!), or assign each family member to grab their own stuff and put it away themselves.

☐ **PILE THE REST.** Even just arranging a messy collection of magazines and letters into one neat stack will provide visual pleasure.

1 Hour

☐ **STOW THE SHOES.** Ask family members to edit their front-door pairs to only one per person. Then place them toe-side down, heel-side up in their bin or neatly on a tray or shoe rack.

☐ **EDIT THE COAT RACK.** So your coat rack has expanded a bit since you first arranged it. Move bulky coats to the closet, and keep only accessories and light jackets hanging on the rack.

☐ **MAKE SENSE OF MAIL.** Finally go through your mail pile. Toss the junk, keep the important bills and invites, and put magazines in their designated basket— or move them to the living room.

☐ **DO A LIGHT CLEANING.** Dust the entryway table, adjusting objects as you go, and give the mirror a quick wipe-down with glass cleaner.

☐ **REPLACE FLOWERS.** After about a week, most buds start to wilt, so out with the old. Rinse out your vase so it's ready for your next farmers' market visit.

A Weekend

☐ **MAKE AN INSTALL.** On a trip to the hardware store, buy a hook for each family member, or purchase a shelf ledge with hooks underneath. (Family photos can rest on the ledge.) Once you've installed them, use a label maker to mark each hook.

☐ **CUT DOWN ON JUNK.** You'll have less mail to organize if you cancel junk mail via the Paperkarma® app, which unsubscribes you from paper mailings.

☐ **COLOR-CODE YOUR HANGERS.** Get into the nitty-gritty and give each family member two hangers in a designated shade for their jackets. (The Container Store sells up to 12 shades, and you can also find more hanger colors online.) Any overflow should go in their personal closets.

☐ **SWITCH SEASONS.** When the front-hall closet begins bursting at the seams with bulky winter wear, it's time to divide everything up into seasons. (What you haven't worn in over a year gets donated.) Zip-top vacuum bags magically transform even the puffiest of parkas into one compact package that's easy to stow. Clean items before storing.

The Elements.. And How To Handle Them In Your Entryway

SAND

Shake or shower off as much as you can before coming in the house. (Quick tip: A sprinkling of baby powder can help remove the sand from your toes and feet because it gets rid of moisture on your skin's surface.) Any grains that make it inside are no match for a vacuum.

SNOW & RAIN

Shake off as much moisture as you can before coming in the house, and leave umbrellas open to dry on the porch or in a mudroom. (Closing them while they're wet can make them rust.) Wipe away any other moisture with a dry mop or a towel.

MUD

It's tempting to want to wipe up wet mud as soon as possible, but letting it dry first makes it easier to clean off floors and fabrics. A broom or vacuum should be able to get dried mud off any kind of floors. For fabric, scrape off what dried bits you can before pre-treating it and throwing it in the washing machine.

Keep It That Way

Because you are constantly coming and going through this room, it's rare that you'd take time to stop and give it a full makeover while you're also rushing out the door or just returning home. It's also not a place where you and the family generally hang out, so it's easy to forget about its clutter when you don't see it for long periods of time. But because it gets so much traffic on a daily basis, it's especially susceptible to getting pretty messy, pretty fast.

Shift Your Mindset

The good news is that while getting organized takes some effort, staying organized requires almost none. "It's all in your attitude," says organizer Andrew Mellen. "It takes the same effort to drop your coat on a chair in the kitchen as it does to hang it up. I've timed it." Think of your new routine as a time-saver, and you're more likely to stick to it.

THE HACK

When you come in from snowy or rainy days with a wet coat, don't hang it on a hook or, worse, in the closet where it can dampen other coats and potentially cause a mold problem. Instead, hang wet clothes in the shower or above a washtub where they can drip dry. Only when they're completely dry should you put them away in the closet.

Take a Vote

Determine if you're going to a be a "no shoes indoors" family or if you're ok with shoes going past the entryway. Either way, it'll decide how often you have to tidy up the shoe pile and mop or vacuum the area surrounding the doorway.

All-Weather Upgrade

Keep any soft pillows or entryway bench cushions free from mud and moisture by using weather-resistant upholstery (like the kind made for outdoor furniture) that won't hold on to moisture and mold. Plus, they're easy to wipe down in the event of a muddy spring day.

Sort the mail. It's easy
to let it pile up, and that's
how important bills, cards,
and invitations get lost in
the shuffle. Plus, it's always
less painful to go through
a daily pile than to do a
weekly sweep.

Outsource the Organizing

Let every family member know that
they're responsible for their own
hook, hanger, or cubby. Announce
this to the fam as a couple, if possible,
and you won't feel like the "bad
organizing cop." Plus, teaching kids
a little responsibility while also
avoiding morning meltdowns—is a
win-win for all.

Erase Scuffs in a Flash

Where there are lots of shoes, there
will be lots of scuff marks. A few
swipes of a Mr. Clean Magic Eraser,
which works on most surfaces, should
make them disappear right away.

Wipe Down the Door Handles

While you're cleaning the entryway,
don't forget to wipe down door handles
with a disinfectant that'll kill any
lingering germs.

Double Down on Mats

Buy a durable, outdoor welcome mat for outside the front
door, and a softer, more eye-friendly one for inside. The
outdoor one will wipe off dirt before you step inside, and
the indoor one will get the last bits. Clean them both once
a week with a good shake to remove dirt. Use a vacuum on
the inside one. For bigger messes, most indoor mats can go
in the laundry machine.

Chapter 2

The Living Room

CREATE A COMFY ATMOSPHERE WHERE YOU CAN JUST SIT BACK AND RELAX.

CREATING A COCOON of coziness starts in the living room, which means it needs to be a space you and your family can really live in. And, well, it can be tough to get your snuggle on with stacks of old magazines dotting the coffee table and toys strewn about the floor. But here's the best news: The living room is an area that everyone in the family inhabits, so that means that everyone in the family is responsible for keeping it tidy. Doling out the duties means you'll get to that "ahhh" feeling even faster.

Your living room is also the perfect place to marry form and function. Sure, you technically need a media console to hold your TV and cable box, but it's also a place to display framed family photos and seashells you collected from your last beach vacation. Bookshelves are utilitarian, but with a little work, they can also be beautiful. Blankets are for warmth, but the just-right combo of throws and pillows makes a personal style statement to whomever comes to visit. Here's how to organize it all for the ultimate peace of mind and body.

Getting into the habit of clearing off your coffee table every night means you'll have an open surface to rest your cup of joe in the morning. (Opposite page) Thoughtfully arranging your bookshelves or media center has a huge visual and mental payoff. Now you can really relax during movie night.

BEFORE YOU CAN SIT BACK AND RELAX IN YOUR COMFY SPACE, YOU'VE GOT TO PUT IN A LITTLE LEGWORK. PLAN A SMART LAYOUT WITH FURNITURE GROUPED SO PEOPLE CAN TALK. ENSURE EVERY SEAT IS WITHIN RANGE OF A COFFEE TABLE OR A SIDE TABLE, AND ADD SOME STORAGE OR SHELVING.

Clean Up Your Coffee Table

It's easy to let magazines, games, and remotes pile up on the tabletop—and then where will the popcorn (or your feet!) go on movie night? Invest in a statement piece that does double duty: A coffee table with a bottom shelf, lid, or drawer gives you a place to store blankets, remotes (stash them on a tray or in a small basket for easy keeping), and a pretty stack of magazines. Ahhh . . . now pass the popcorn.

Manage Your Media Center

Thankfully, TVs have gotten slimmer and DVD collections are (mostly) a thing of the past. But that doesn't mean that your console cords and random knickknacks won't distract you during your next Netflix binge. Think of your media center as divided into zones: lower shelves and cupboards can fit boxes to house the few sentimental DVDs you're still holding onto, and higher shelves are for framed family photos and mini sculptures. Bonus: When each shelf has an assigned purpose, putting things back is a breeze.

Hide Your TV Cords

Avoid getting wires crossed by purchasing cord ties or the plastic zip ties that professional cable installers use. They're not only incredibly cheap, they're also super-effective. Zip-tie the cables together, then use sharp scissors to cut off the tie's slack down to the nub. Next step: ID each cord by giving it a tag. Cords can become a tangled mess when you unplug the devices and the wires slip behind the furniture, even when they're zip-tied, so use adhesive cable clips to hold each in place.

Corral Your Stuff

A large wicker basket is your living room's best friend. Stock pillows and fold blankets or roll them to fit vertically, so you can see all the items in your cozy arsenal. Anything that doesn't make it into the basket gets exiled. For hidden storage, a lidded bench or ottoman can hold soft items that you want within reach but won't be needing year-round.

See the Light

Cut down on visual clutter with a long-armed floor lamp that can swing over the sofa when the sun goes down or shed some light over a cozy reading chair. Having a versatile lighting option also means you won't have to swap it out when you get the redecorating itch.

Up Your Game

Board games can be bulky, and the mangled cardboard boxes can be an eyesore on living room shelves. A neater way to contain the fun: Slot a dozen of them into a hanging fabric organizer in a hall closet. Or, if you have the room, try plastic Game Savers storage units, which hold the boards and accessories to recent editions (1999 and later) of Clue, Sorry!, Parcheesi, Stratego, and more.

Downsize Your Side Tables

It's a universal organizing truth that the bigger the side table, the more clutter it will collect. Choose one with enough surface area to fit a table lamp plus a little extra room for a book or a cup of coffee. Keeping it simple also means fewer places to set things (like your glasses), so you won't have to go searching for them later.

Give Yourself an Out

Let's be real: You can't have everything in its place every moment of the day. But you can cut down on wayward stuff by giving it a defined space. Place a storage ottoman or large seagrass basket in a corner of the living room to stow plush toys or that random sweatshirt when you don't have time to run them upstairs. Just commit to a deadline (say, the next morning, when you're having coffee) to put back the items.

Furniture With Hidden Storage

No one will be able to tell where you've stashed your things.

L-SHAPED SOFA

The long side of some L-shaped sofas lifts to reveal a hiding place for extra-large blankets that won't fit on the sofa.

OTTOMANS

Lift the lid, and you've got an instant spot to store a lightweight throw.

COFFEE TABLE

Find one with a lid that opens to reveal a place for a laptop, magazines, reading glasses, or slim books.

BOOKS

A secret storage book, which you can buy online, is made from a recycled volume with the center of some pages removed. Tuck the remote inside.

4 Simple Rules for Decorating Any Type of Living Room

1

PICK ELEMENTS THAT SPEAK TO ONE ANOTHER.

The best way to give a room good flow is to choose pieces that coordinate in some way without being matchy-matchy. If you have a brass chandelier, add a bronze bowl on the coffee table, or choose a sofa pillow with one color that's like a shade in the rug.

2

VARY THE SHAPES.

If you have mostly squarish pieces in a room, it can feel one-note. Swap in some softer or rounded accents—an end table, a lamp, an ottoman, a glazed ceramic object— to offset the other elements.

3

LAYER YOUR LIGHTING.

Just because you have overheads doesn't mean you're set with lighting. A good rule of thumb is to add at least one floor lamp and one table lamp to brighten up the space and make it functional for reading.

4

YOU CAN'T GO WRONG WITH A PAIR OF POUFS.

Low seating, such as poufs, stools, or ottomans, is easy to move around for whenever you have extra guests.

Blanket and Pillow Pattern Combos That Work

ZIGZAG

+

STRIPES

ZEBRA STRIPES

+

CHEETAH SPOTS

FLORAL

+

GINGHAM

IKAT

+

POLKA DOT

"A universal remote is great to have on hand in your living room. Instead of keeping track of multiple remotes to operate the television, DVR, sound system, and DVD player, a single remote reduces clutter."

—ERIN ROONEY DOLAND, ORGANIZER AND
EDITOR IN CHIEF OF TUMBLEWEED.LIFE
AND EDITOR-AT-LARGE AT UNCLUTTERER.COM

Organize This

A PRETTY <u>BOOKCASE</u> GIVES YOUR TOMES A HAPPY HOME.

ARRANGE BY CONVENIENCE, NOT COLOR

There's no denying that a rainbow-stacked library is beautiful, but it's not the best system when you need to grab the astronomy book when homework is due or you are looking for your favorite cookbook while the Bolognese is burning on the stove. Sort your books by subject or by which ones you'll want most available when you need them.

ROCK ON

If you don't own traditional bookends, use large, smooth stones or rocks to keep books in line on a shelf while also adding an earthy vibe. Or, lay a few books in a horizontal stack to keep the standing stack from falling over.

GO HORIZONTAL

You'll fit the most books on a bookshelf by lining them up vertically, but a few horizontal stacks (larger art books work best) can add interest and be a tiny platform for framed photos or pretty objects.

CONTAIN YOURSELF

Not everything is display-worthy. Put loose photos, manuals, and errant phone chargers in colorful boxes or baskets. Store them on the bottom shelf or in cabinets.

The Tools

SOFA

CHAIRS

SMALL SIDE TABLES

BASKETS

FLOOR LAMP
(LONG-ARM)

ORGANIZING ESSENTIAL

This goes-with-anything piece looks like a simple enough coffee table, but its top lifts up to reveal tons of storage space within. Genius.

REMOTE CONTROL TRAY

DECORATIVE BOXES

They're not just pretty faces. Stylish boxes are smart places to store remotes, coasters, or reading glasses.

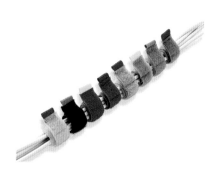

VELCRO CORD HOLDERS

Wrap these Velcro ties around cable box and TV cords to keep everything together. They're like cable ties, but no scissors required.

Small-Space Solutions

WHILE THERE'S NO DEBATING THAT YOU NEED AN
INVITING SPACE FOR LOUNGING, SIPPING COCKTAILS
WITH FRIENDS, AND TV BINGING, THERE IS A THING
AS TOO COZY. HERE'S HOW TO MAKE THE BEST OUT
OF A TINY LIVING ROOM AREA.

Nix the Coffee Table

No really, it's fine to forgo a clunky table if you've got solid side tables, which take up less room than one that sits in front of the furniture. Or, if you just can't give up on one, go for a slim bench or an acrylic table that seems almost invisible.

Make Use of Corners

Corners are often overlooked as versatile spaces. They're the perfect nooks for beanbags, stools, or reading chairs.

Be Pic-y

Instead of crowding precious surface space with picture frames, print out your favorite snaps (or upload your Instagrams) at socialprintstudio.com and create a photo display on your wall. Neon masking or decorative washi tape is a fun (and deposit-safe) way to attach images directly to the wall; try using framing wire and S-hooks to hang them; or just adhere Bulldog clips or repurposed CD jewel cases to create a quick-change display.

Make Floating Shelves Your Friend

Big bookcases can feel heavy. A more airy option? Floating shelves that offer storage but take up less space than furniture. Plus, you can play with height: Line the top of your wall with books to get them up and out of the way while still making a decorative statement.

Get Reflective

Hang or place a large mirror opposite your window. It'll bounce light all around your living room, giving it a bright feel. Metallic accessories, like bronze figurines and silver candlesticks, give off a similar glow.

Cover Up Cord Clutter

For a small space, consider a media console with cabinet doors. It hides cords and is a great place to also stash board games, DVDs you can't part with, and books, all without adding visual clutter to your hangout.

The Real Simple Method Checklist

IF YOU HAVE . . .

15 Minutes

☐ **MOVE THE BIG STUFF.** Sweaters, toys, and snack bowls need to go back to their homes in a flash. Throw anything else into hidden storage, like drawers and benches.

☐ **CLEAR THE TABLES.** Uncluttered surfaces make a room look instantly organized. Place books and magazines in piles on the bottom shelves of your coffee table and side tables.

1 Hour

☐ **ROLL AWAY.** Fold your blankets flat, then roll them like cinnamon bun dough, and place them vertically in a basket. Using this system means you'll see your entire stash at a glance, and any ones that don't fit can be put in another room.

☐ **WHITTLE DOWN THE MAGAZINE PILE.** Recycle any monthly magazines older than two months, and weeklies past two weeks. (But archive the *Real Simple* magazines, of course! We kid.) Newspapers older than a week have got to go, too.

☐ **FLUFF THE PILLOWS.** Sounds silly, but just readjusting the stuffing inside your pillows and arranging them anew on the sofa can make the room look tidy.

A Weekend

☐ **TACKLE THOSE BOOKSHELVES.**
Take a day to measure your shelves
and shop for bins that will fit along
the bottom. Then, take everything
off the shelves (except for your TV if
your shelves surround it), and put it
on the floor. Start with your books,
arranging them back on the shelves
by subject, and donate what won't fit.
Then, move on to the bottom shelf
bins, throwing in extra items that you
don't want visible. Finally, add picture
frames and decorative objects to the
remaining shelves.

☐ **BOARD UP THE GAMES.** Open
each game and take inventory of
missing pieces. If a game is missing
so many pieces that it's unplayable,
it's time to toss it and get a new version.
But if you're just missing a Monopoly
character, replace it with a small toy or
trinket from the junk drawer.

☐ **ROUND UP THE CORDS.** Dig behind
the console so you can zip-tie and
color-code all the TV and DVD player
(and Apple TV and stereo and gaming
system) cords so that they're in neat
bundles. The next time you replace an
electronic device, it'll be a cinch.

☐ **TAKE STOCK OF YOUR HIDDEN
INVENTORY.** Hidden storage is
genius because it makes clutter
disappear in a flash, but it also means
you don't often get to see all the things
you've been stowing. Take some
time to go through what's stored, and
determine what you use on a regular
basis. If you find yourself saying, "Oh,
wow, I had no idea we still had this!,"
then it's time to donate or toss.

Ask the Organizer

Q: Where should I draw the line at how many keepsakes to keep?

A: Mementos have one of two purposes: to display or to save. Cramming something onto a cluttered shelf is a sign to let go of it. Items that you want to save—personal letters, a ribbon from third grade—need physical limitations. Give each family member an airtight container to keep on a high closet shelf.

—ERIN ROONEY DOLAND, ORGANIZER AND
EDITOR IN CHIEF OF TUMBLEWEED.LIFE
AND EDITOR-AT-LARGE AT UNCLUTTERER.COM

Gallery Wall 101

ALL YOU NEED IS AN AFTERNOON TO ARTFULLY DECORATE
THE SPACE ABOVE YOUR SOFA. TRY ANY OF THESE SETUPS.

A Uniformed Grid

Before hanging any
frames, trace each one
onto newspaper, and play
around with the cutouts
taped to the wall until
you find a setup that
feels well-proportioned.
Put some of your biggest,
boldest pieces below,
lining up their bottom
edges. Build up vertical
columns from there.

An Easy Collage

Using frames and mats
in a simple colorway
unifies all the artwork
in this setup, giving
the collection an
orderly look even with
a few unframed items
sprinkled in. Start with
one piece somewhere
in the middle. Then,
aiming for balance,
build up, down,
and out. Haphazard
spacing—two inches
separating some pieces,
four or five between
others—lends an
organic, easygoing look.
Ignore the old-school
"eye level" hanging
rule and let the artwork
explode downward. It
makes for a fresh and
dynamic display.

An Ever-Changing Collection

There's no measuring
or hammering needed
with an ultra-adaptable,
picture-ledge display
that lets you add pieces
or shift them around
when you want. Position
the frames so they're
overlapping slightly in an
uneven way. The goal: a
silhouette of undulating
heights. A picture ledge
that's 3½ inches deep
is enough to layer two
framed pieces.

**INEXPENSIVE
ONLINE
ART FINDS**

20x200.com
Tappan Collective
theposters.co
minted.com

Keep It That Way

Your living room gets so much daily play that keeping it organized can seem like a constant battle. It's also such a versatile spot—a playground, a reading nook, and a place to entertain—that it helps to do a little sweep-through every day so it's always in order when you're ready to relax.

IF YOU DO ONE THING EVERY DAY

Clear off the coffee table. When it's free of clutter, you'll be able to enjoy movie night (and just Tuesday night) even more.

Time Yourself

The easiest way to maintain an organized living room is to give it a little attention every day or so. Set a timer for five minutes and instruct everyone in the house to do as much as they can in that timeframe to reset the space. Do it earlier in the evening rather than later, so you have energy and won't put it off to surf the Internet. You'll be surprised how much you can accomplish in such a short amount of time.

Take Snaps

Once your living room magic is done, take a picture of your media consoles and bookshelves so that you can admire your hard work—and also so you'll have a reference when it comes time to tidy up.

Keep Your Library Under Control

As you begin to add new books to your collection, follow the one-in, one-out rule. Any outtakes go straight to a friend, donation center, or library.

Clean Your Furniture

When you have a few extra minutes, tackle a little cleaning. For hard surfaces, the method you use depends on the item's finish.

ACRYLIC

Dampen a cloth with water and a little dishwashing liquid. Wring it out, and wipe the furniture from top to bottom. Avoid solvents, ammonia, and vinegar, all of which can dissolve the coating or finish.

ANTIQUE WOOD

Wet a cloth with distilled water, and wring it out well, as excess water can warp wood. Wipe the piece in long strokes from top to bottom. Buff with a clean cloth.

HARD FINISHES (LACQUER, POLYURETHANE) AND PAINTED WOOD

Dust the furniture from top to bottom with a microfiber cloth. Mix one teaspoon of dishwashing liquid with one gallon of water, dampen a cloth with the solution, then wring it out. Wipe the piece of furniture from top to bottom.

OIL FINISHES

Dust the entire piece from top to bottom with a microfiber cloth. Douse a clean cloth with odorless mineral spirits (a solvent sold at hardware stores that thins oil finishes and removes grime). Wipe from top to bottom.

SHELLAC AND VARNISH FINISHES

Dust the piece from top to bottom with a microfiber cloth. Dampen another cloth with mineral spirits, and rub the surface in circular strokes from top to bottom. Or, use a cloth that has been dipped in a solution of one teaspoon of dishwashing liquid and one gallon of water, then wrung out well.

WICKER

Vacuum the surface from top to bottom with a brush attachment. Mix two tablespoons of dishwashing liquid in a bucket of cool water. Dip in a cloth, and wring it out very well. Wipe the piece from top to bottom. For a deeper cleaning, call a professional.

And Eliminate Those Sofa Stains

For softer items, like couches and ottomans, take into consideration what cloth they're cut from. That'll determine how to clean it.

LEATHER AND VINYL

Vacuum the piece of furniture on a low setting with a brush attachment. Rub soiled areas with a microfiber cloth that is slightly dampened with water. Water can remove dirt but won't permanently discolor the leather. For deeper cleaning, call a professional upholstery cleaner.

PILE FABRICS (CHENILLE AND CORDUROY) AND WOOL

Vacuum the piece on a low setting with an upholstery attachment using long, horizontal strokes from top to bottom. Do not use the vacuum's hard-bristle attachment because it can pull on fabric. For deeper cleaning, call a professional.

SUEDE

Clean suede using a product recommended by the manufacturer. Avoid using any moisture on suede because it will permanently stain. For deeper cleaning, call a professional.

SLIPCOVERS

For cotton and linen, remove the covers and machine-wash them on a delicate setting following the care instruction on the label, which is usually attached near the zipper. For silk, handwash the covers in a sink filled with warm water and a capful of delicate laundry detergent. Or, have the cover dry-cleaned.

CANVAS, JACQUARD, AND RAYON

Run a dry-cleaning sponge over the fabric in short, even strokes to lift ingrained dirt. Be gentle on jacquard, since delicate yarns can pull and snag. Add two capfuls of mild detergent to a bucket of cool water. Dip in a sponge or cloth, wring it out well, and go back and forth over the fabric with long strokes. Use as little liquid as possible, since wet fabric can sprout mildew. Let the pieces air-dry.

Power Up Your Electronics

TV

A dusty TV is no bueno. Clean the screens of plasma, LCD, and standard television sets in long, horizontal strokes, beginning at the top of the screen, with a dry electrostatic dust-mop cloth or a dry-cleaning sponge. (Shorter strokes cause smudging.) Wipe the casing of the set with an electrostatic dust-mop cloth lightly spritzed with glass cleaner. To remove stubborn dirt, purchase a specialty screen wipe, and follow the package instructions.

REMOTES

Wipe the entire surface of a remote with a disinfecting wipe. For sticky patches, dip a cotton swab in rubbing alcohol, pinch out or away the excess moisture with your fingers, and circle the sides and tops of the buttons to dissolve grime.

SPEAKERS

Dust the entire surface of the stereo, including the knobs, by wiping everything with an electrostatic dust-mop cloth that has been slightly dampened with water and a few drops of dishwashing liquid, then wrung out. Then run a clean medium-sized paintbrush with soft, natural bristles over the speakers from left to right to lift dust.

THE HACK

Open and close your window treatments (blinds, curtains, shades) every few days to displace dust from the fabric. When it falls to the floor, just run a dust mop over the surface.

Don't Forget the Lights

No matter the material, wipe the base of your lamps with a cloth dampened with water. For shades, vacuum them on a low setting with a brush attachment in long, vertical strokes. To clean a fabric shade, roll it from side to side in a tub filled with a few inches of lukewarm water and two capfuls of delicate laundry detergent. Rinse with a damp cloth, and gently blot the inside and outside with a white or colorfast towel. Lay the towel on the floor, and set the shade on it right-side up to dry.

YOUR MONTHLY CLEANING CHECKLIST

☐ Dust the moldings

☐ Dust the door frames and jambs

☐ Vacuum the heating and AC vents

☐ Wipe down the switch plates and the doorknobs with a soapy cloth

Chapter 3

The Kitchen

WHIP UP SOMETHING GREAT IN EVERYONE'S FAVORITE SPACE.

WHETHER YOU COOK EVERY DAY or you're more of a special-occasion chef, arranging the right setup for your workspace is the first step to any great recipe, no matter how major or minor the meal. Without a well-thought-out setting, important tools disappear, and well-intentioned sous chefs can't find what they need. But in a cleverly organized space, the work just flows. Making items visible and accessible means it'll be easier for whoever's making breakfast to do it in less time and with less hassle.

Keep in mind that your kitchen isn't just utilitarian. If the growing popularity of open floor plans with spacious islands is any indication, a kitchen is also a popular hangout during parties (it's usually where the apps are, after all) or on weeknights before the food hits the table. Making it an inviting spot gets the good vibes going right away. Dotting clutter-free counters with a few entertaining treats—small bowls of chips or veggies with dip—can transform your go-to cooking spot into a place that no one will want to leave. Here's how to make the heart of your home work for you.

Keep open shelving neat and airy. Fill clear bins with dry goods for a display that's as practical as it is pretty. (Opposite page) Show off your space-saving skills. Hang coffee mugs from hooks, and use shelf risers for bowls so you don't have to lift a stack to get to the plates.

THE KEY TO AN ULTRA FUNCTIONAL SPACE IS KNOWING WHERE TO FIND EVERYTHING. PUT LIKE WITH LIKE, AND KEEP ALL THE ESSENTIALS WITHIN ARM'S REACH. THEN STORE AWAY ITEMS YOU DON'T NEED ON A DAILY BASIS—BUT MAKE SURE THEY'RE STILL EASY TO FIND WHEN THE HOLIDAYS HIT.

Make Countertop Magic

With a little rearranging, you can make everything on your countertop work for you. After all, you don't want to waste precious time during dinner prep looking for things. Make a place in the hot zone (around the stove and sink) for the essentials: oil, vinegar, knives, cutting board. Move special-occasion cookware, like a fondue pot, out of cabinets in the zone so that what's left can be neatly organized and easily spotted. And don't just place ingredients and tools where they seem to fit. Instead, think about where you will be using them. Keep the basket of potatoes near the cutting board, the sugar and flour near the stand mixer, and your best-loved pan on the front burner.

Fix the Fridge Door

A clean fridge, free of photos and papers can seriously open a room. It's almost like adding a window.

Rethink Your Servingware

Serving pieces like cake stands and serving bowls can still be put to work when you're not entertaining. A cake stand can hold spices and oils and lift them off the counter while you're cooking. Or, a salad bowl can store fresh fruit when it's not being used at dinnertime. Putting them on display also saves precious cabinet space.

Keep Your Tools Close at Hand

Instead of panicking when you can't find a whisk when the béarnaise begins to boil, stash your most-used items in an easy-to-reach container next to the stove. Wooden spoons, tongs, a ladle, and spatulas can all find a home there. Or, add hooks to a pot rack to give slotted spoons a home.

Free Up Drawers

Measuring spoons, whisks, and pot holders are the types of tools that jam up kitchen drawers. Instead of cramming them in, hang them on adhesive hooks on the insides of cabinet doors. Just make sure to position the hooks in the spaces between the shelves so the doors can close properly. For everything else, add an expandable insert with adjustable compartments, and then fill the insert strategically: gadgets you use the most in front and the rest in back.

Hang Only Essential Pots

A good frying pan, a saucepan, a large sauté pan, a cast-iron skillet, and a stockpot will handle the majority of your needs. Hang everything except the stockpot from a small ceiling-mounted rack or pegboard. Displaying pots and pans means you'll want to keep them looking fresh and clean with a gentle abrasive cleaner like Bar Keepers Friend. Oh, and because cutting boards are a pain to store, buy a hangable one and add it to the hanging pans.

"File" Away Your Cookware

Instead of shoving skillets and lids in wherever they fit (cabinet chaos!), store them in a pan rack or organizer. It can also keep sheet pans and cutting boards in check and upright.

Use Under-Cabinet Space

Under-cabinet lighting strips (attached with screws or double-stick Velcro) keep the focus on the onions at hand. A battery-operated version won't dangle a cord or steal an outlet from the microwave. An under-shelf cookbook holder pulls down when you need it and folds up when you don't.

Make the Right Cut

Protect knives, and your fingers, with individual knife guards so that you can stack them next to each other without damaging them. Ideally, store them flat in a drawer separate from other silverware. A wall-mounted magnetic strip near where you're going to be doing your chopping is also a good option. If you like the look of a knife block, buy one where the slots are horizontal, as in parallel to the counter rather than perpendicular. Resting them on the blade's edges can dull them over time.

Put Dishes in Plain Sight

Short on cupboard space? Get things out in the open. Display everyday dishes against a well-marked chalkboard wall. The dark backdrop allows you to clearly (and creatively) indicate a home for each item, encouraging others (as in not just you!) to help restock once the dishwasher is finished. Draw outlines of shapely pieces if you're the artistic type, or just say it like it is with words.

Toss Missing Tupperware Parts

Purge ruthlessly, keeping only containers you use all the time. Toss anything missing a top or a bottom. Split the space with a drawer divider to impose order: glass on one side, plastic on the other. Tuck the biggest glass piece in one corner, and find snug spaces for all other angular glassware; then, slip round pieces in last. Leave tops on glass containers, and stack pieces (don't nest—glass might stick together and break). Nest plastics, storing sideways if upright is too high for the drawer. Store plastic tops separate from their bases since a seal can create a stale smell.

Or Consider This Cabinet Trick

Shelves stay neater if you divide cabinets into categories (everyday plates in one, most-used cookware in another). Walk yourself through your usual kitchen routine and consider how many steps you're taking from a cabinet to its corresponding task. If a switch-up will shorten the distance, do it.

Put the Walls to Work

Create a nonfridge spot for schedules or artwork, like a magnetic board. Oversize Post-it Notes or hanging rolls of paper, which you can find at a stationery or an art-supply store, are also useful for jotting down reminders. Simply tear them off when it's time to shop or move on to your next great idea.

Keep Party Gear Handy

When it's time to entertain, create a place for platters and trays—with dividers to maintain order—so you don't have to hunt for them while the bruschetta turns soggy. Give candles, place mats, and other table toppers a dedicated drawer. Use an index card box to store recipes, past menus, friends' food preferences, or wine labels. (Soak a bottle to remove the label, let it dry, paste it on an index card, and jot down tasting notes.)

Make Your Vase Supply Vanish

You need only three kinds of vases: a bud vase for one or two stems; a cup-shaped vessel for small bouquets; and a cylindrical vase for bunches of long-stemmed flowers. But if you like a larger collection, nestle vases inside one another with a paper towel between them so they don't rattle. And never store them under the kitchen sink where they can easily be knocked over. Instead, put them up on a shelf where they're better protected.

Make Recycling & Composting Efficient, Too

Having a bin for compost and one for bottles and cans right next to the regular trash, instead of out in the garage or in the mudroom, streamlines end-of-meal cleanup. Speaking of trash, line the bin with four or five bags in one go, so the task of taking out the trash is a breeze. When you notice the receptacle getting full, you can snatch the top bag on your way out of the room without needing to dig through the pantry for a replacement.

Think Seasonally

Tweak organization according to the season. In the fall and winter, keep your Dutch oven on the stove and a basket of soup ingredients at the ready in the pantry. In the summer, when you're always reaching for your blender and water pitchers, move them front and center.

Go Under the Kitchen Sink

Oh the irony of having messy cleaning supplies, right? Make sure the cabinet under the sink doesn't turn into the Bermuda Triangle by making a small investment in a pull-out organizer. That way, sponges and supplies don't get lost in the back behind the pipes. You'll be able to see all "of your cleaning products at a glance and can grab them even faster when messes happen.

Pretty Up Your Pantry

Organized people think in zones. Arrange things by usage rather than type. In the pantry, group breakfast items: pancake mix, syrup, nut butters, jams. Use airtight, stackable containers to arrange dry foods, and add a canned-food storage rack, especially if your shelves are deep and wide. See-through containers allow you to quickly see what you have (and how much).

Keep Your Condiments and Spices in Order

Consider a two-tier Lazy Susan, which fits on a cupboard shelf and features a tray that can fit bottles of ketchup or vinegar. Store spices on the Lazy Susan or in a drawer. Transfer them from various spice jars to uniform containers, and mark each with a label.

Rearrange Your Library

Organize your cookbooks in a way that reflects your own inner logic and tastes. It may make sense to alphabetize one section by author, create another section for a favorite ingredient (tomatoes, lemons, herbs) or theme (barbecue, dessert), and a third by region. One shelf could be arranged by world cuisines while another goes from breakfast to dessert. Just don't keep your books over the stove or sink where they could absorb humidity.

Round Up Your Recipes

Take the notecards stuffed in the front covers of your favorite cookbooks and scan them. Then catalog them using online tools or apps like Evernote, Paprika Recipe Manager, Basil, or Eat Your Books. This will allow you to save, categorize, search, and even add notes for your favorite recipes. Or, if you're old-school, buy an accordion binder where you can store the cards by course (appetizers, mains, sides, and desserts).

Take a Big Step Up

Pop quiz: What's in your highest kitchen cabinets? Odds are, the highest shelves are either empty or storing something you've either forgotten about or don't really need. A stepladder can be a kitchen MVP so that you can utilize all your room's space.

"Keep countertops clutter-free by storing only things that you use at least a couple of times a week, like the coffeemaker, a utensil crock, and a small tray with your go-to oils, vinegars, and salt and pepper. One exception? A big stand mixer, which can be too heavy to easily move. Tuck it in a black hole corner of a countertop beneath a cabinet where it's out of the way. But if you never bake, give it away. Even if it was a wedding present!"

—LISA ZASLOW, ORGANIZER, FOUNDER OF GOTHAM ORGANIZERS

Organize This

MAKE YOUR DAILY DIVE INTO THE
REFRIGERATOR A TREAT.

PUT LIKE WITH LIKE

A good rule of thumb: Group similar items together. Designate a shelf for beverages (and use a can organizer to keep them in line) or a spot where all dairy products should live to make them easy to find.

MAKE SPACE FOR PREPPED ITEMS

Once a week, cut up fresh produce to have on hand for snacks and mealtime. Stash it at eye level in stackable, clear, airtight containers; then grab and go.

PACK THE FREEZER SMART

Make designated sections (prepared meals, vegetables, desserts). Use dividers or multilayer ice caddies to keep containers neat and accessible, and label everything.

DESIGNATE YOUR DOORS

The storage space on the door should be used to stash condiments and sauces. That frees up shelf space, which stays cooler, for more perishable items.

CREATE INSTANT ORDER

Reduce shelf clutter (and avoid losing items in the back of the fridge) by employing acrylic bins to corral awkward-shaped packages, like yogurt pouches or deli meat.

USE FLEXIBLE LABELS

Make the contents easy to identify at a glance by labeling bins with chalk markers.

DON'T FORGET YOU CAN ADJUST THE
SHELVES SO YOUR BIG BOTTLE OF COLD-BREW
COFFEE DOESN'T HAVE TO LIE ON ITS SIDE.

The Tools

SHELF RISER

SLIDING SHELVES

You'll never wonder what hidden appliance or pot is lingering in the back of your bottom cabinets ever again.

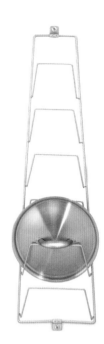

LID RACK

PAN ORGANIZER

PARTITIONED TRAY

Prevent utensil pileup and make use of every inch of drawer space with an expandable divided insert.

STACKABLE BASKETS

RECYCLING BIN

TRASH CAN

DOOR ORGANIZER

The mighty Lazy Susan is a game changer in the kitchen. Use it in the pantry for spices, in shelves for coffee mugs, or on the counter near the stove for cooking oils.

AIRTIGHT, CLEAR, SQUARE CONTAINERS

LABELS

Wondering how old those leftovers are? From freezer storage to shelving, use labels that say what everything is. Reusable dry-erase tape makes this necessity even easier.

CLEAR PLASTIC BINS

MONTANA JARS

Small-Space Solutions

EVEN TINY KITCHENS REQUIRE SO MUCH STUFF. AVOID DROWNING IN POTS AND PANS WITH THESE TRICKS FOR KEEPING IT ALL TOGETHER.

Buy a Floating Island

A rolling cart with a wooden cutting-board top and drawers down below is a genius way to add countertop space wherever you need it. Store utensils in the drawers, use the top as a prep space, and roll the cart away (and use it as a mini bar cart) when it's not needed in the kitchen.

Utilize Your Walls

Mount your dishwashing rack on the wall to clear up countertop space near the sink. Install grids, pegs, or rails to hang utensils and dish towels.

Look Up

Fruit bowls are pretty, but they take up precious counter space. Instead, hang your produce in a three-tier wire fruit basket where it will be on display but out of the way.

Hang Dry Goods

Mount Mason jar lids underneath your cabinets and fill the jars with dried pasta, pretzels, and popcorn kernels. Then lift the jars into the lids and rotate the jars to secure them into the lids. Suddenly you've got a chic floating display that won't clutter up your space.

Stick Your Spices

Fill magnetic tins with spices, label them with a permanent marker, and place them on the side of your fridge. It's also a great way to take inventory before starting a recipe and realizing you're out of cinnamon.

Use the Doors

Install a rack or organizer on walls or inside pantry or cabinet doors.

The Real Simple Method Checklist

IF YOU HAVE . . .

15 Minutes

☐ **HIDE WHAT YOU CAN**. This is not the time for an overhaul. Throw dirty dishes in the dishwasher; heck, throw anything in the dishwasher, as long as you remember not to turn it on. Then, use the pantry to store cabinet overflow and random bags of snack foods that were out on the counter before a surprise guest announced they were on their way over in about 15.

☐ **WIPE DOWN SURFACES**. A sparkling countertop makes the whole room look spiffy.

1 Hour

☐ **EDIT YOUR KITCHEN DRAWER**. It takes mere minutes to round up duplicate tools. Test them all, keep the one that works best, then donate or toss the rest. Extra credit: Move rarely used pieces (turkey baster, melon baller) to a bin on a high shelf.

☐ **PARE DOWN THE PANTRY**. Toss any expired foods, and consolidate doubles into one container. As you're slimming down your supply, store like items with like to avoid doubling up again.

☐ **CLEAR OFF COUNTERTOP SPACE**. Move any appliances you don't use every day (food processor, blender, toaster) to bottom shelves so they're not taking up precious prep-work space.

A Weekend

☐ **FIX YOUR FRIDGE.** It's time to invest in clear bins for your food items so you can see exactly what you have at any given moment. In that same spirit, pull out the crisper drawer if it's possible with your model. The minute that thing is closed, it's like the food in there doesn't exist because you're not seeing it. Without the drawer, you have a nice, open shelf that keeps items visible, prompting you to use them. The same logic goes for food-storage containers. Get rid of the large yogurt tubs or opaque lidded bowls you use for leftovers. If you're not seeing what's inside, you're likely to forget about what's in them. Invest in a uniform set of clear glass containers—square or rectangular ones take up less space than round ones.

☐ **PICK APART THE PANTRY.** Remove everything and wipe down the shelves. Then, organize items in clear jars or plastic boxes, arranged by food type. (Pastas in one, beans in another.) Stash the stuff you reach for most often at eye level.

☐ **PICK YOUR FAVE POTS AND PANS.** Chances are, you don't use every pot or pan in the 10-piece set you bought, and it's easy to stockpile saucepans without realizing it. Sift through your collection and keep only the ones you use on a regular basis. (If one looks too clean, it's probably not one you use often.) Edit your collection, wash your faves, and hang them up. Donate the rest, or give them to a niece or nephew on their way to college.

Dishwasher Do's and Don'ts

FORK TINES UP OR DOWN? PLATES FACING RIGHT OR LEFT? WELCOME TO YOUR ULTIMATE DISH-LOADING DIRECTIVES.

Do

Run the Dishwasher at Night

Some utility companies charge more at peak usage times, and night is a less demanding time, so it can lower your bills.

Do

Organize Utensils

Sorting by type is a time-saver for unloading. Put forks with forks and knives with knives, with handles facing up to avoid getting poked or punctured when you take them out. Spoons will stay dirty if they're "spooning," so insert some with handles facing down (or separate them in a slotted holder).

Do

Make a Game Plan

You'll use the space best if you first scan the kitchen and form a loading strategy, like putting big pieces in first and filling in with the smaller ones. When in doubt, take something out. If pieces are overlapping or keeping the spray arms from spinning, they won't get clean.

Don't

Face Plates All in the Same Direction

Instead, place them on the bottom rack facing inward toward the spray arms, with smaller plates in front of large ones, so the spray can reach all of them.

Don't

Rinse Plates

Prerinsing wastes water and isn't necessary if you run the machine within a day. And today's machines can handle food residue. One exception is rice, which is worth rinsing off because it can clog the drain hose.

Don't

Unload from Top to Bottom

A piece on the upper rack may have a pool of water, so if you unload the top rack first, the water can spill onto dry dishes below.

Q: What's the best system to keep my kitchen sink items in order?

A: The neater this area is, the less likely you are to consider dishwashing a chore. Use a sponge holder that suction cups inside the edge of the sink so your sponge drips dry neatly. Also, decanting dishwashing liquid and hand soap into matching pump dispensers is a pretty way to keep your space looking intact. The final step? Add a hook to keep a dish towel close at hand.

—LISA ZASLOW, ORGANIZER, FOUNDER OF GOTHAM ORGANIZERS

Keep It That Way

The good news about keeping your kitchen in order is that it's a space you use every day, so there's less of a chance of you creating a system and not sticking to it. Still, there are a few tricks to maintaining your organizational masterpiece.

Plan It All Out

When it comes to keeping the fridge organized, meal planning (weekly or half-weekly) is super important. Buy food for specific meals or recipes so that you know pretty much exactly when you're going to use it. Replenish pantry staples as needed.

Put Away Your Haul

It can be tempting to quickly put groceries away once you get home from shopping—who doesn't want to just shove everything randomly in cabinets and move on with life? But you made this new system for a reason, so take care to put items away in their designated places. That way, the next time you need to find the rice, you won't have to call on a search party.

Make Labels

Using labels to assign out shelving doesn't just help you in the short run, it also instructs the family (and thoughtful visitors) on where to put things back when they're done using them. Plus, putting labels in your pantry is another easy way to take inventory of what you need to add to the grocery list when stock runs low.

End on a High Note

When you get to the end of the recipe, don't stop when the cooking is done—take time to put away your ingredients, wash pots, and wipe down the counter. Even just cleaning your prep items while the main dish is in the oven is an easy way to keep your kitchen sanity.

IF YOU DO ONE THING EVERY DAY

Clear off the countertop. Not only will you love the look of wide open spaces, but putting together your next meal will be a total breeze because the first step won't involve finding homes for loose mail and your garlic press.

Stick to a Cleaning Routine

This seven-step weekly cleaning plan means you won't panic when a friend stops by and stays for dinner.

1

Going in the direction of the grain, wipe cabinet fronts from top to bottom with a microfiber cloth dampened with water and a few drops of mild cleaner. Rinse the cloth, wring it out well, and repeat without the cleaner, taking care to remove cleaner residue that can dull the finish.

2

Wipe the stovetop with a microfiber cloth moistened with water and cleaner.

3

Wet a microfiber cloth with water and mild cleaner, and wipe the countertops in a circular motion. To get rid of the soap film, mist the entire area with water from a spray bottle and wipe it down again with a clean cloth. Wash the tile backsplash using the same method, scrubbing any food splatters from the grout.

4

Wipe the outside of the refrigerator, the dishwasher, and the microwave.

5

Disinfect the garbage can by spraying all-purpose cleaner on both the inside and the outside of the bin and wiping it with a clean cloth.

6

With cloth and cleaner, scrub the sink basin in a circular motion from the top to the drain. Use an old toothbrush to remove any mold lurking in the edges of the drain and the faucet. Rinse the entire area with water, and wipe it down with a clean cloth to bring out its shine.

7

Sweep the floor with a broom using long strokes and working from the walls to the middle of the room. Try not to lift up the broom at the end of each stroke or dust will be kicked into the air. Make several piles of debris as you go, picking them up with a dustpan and dumping them in the garbage. To clean corners, blow out the dust with a hairdryer, then sweep up or vacuum using a crevice attachment to reach tight spots and underneath cabinet bases.

THE HACK

Stash extra trash bags at the bottom of your kitchen garbage can. With a clean supply at the ready, swapping in a new bag is less of a chore.

Chapter 4

The Dining Room

ADD A LITTLE JOY TO EVERY MEAL.

IN A PERFECT WORLD, the dining room would be a place for dining—and dining only. But you know how it works: One minute it's a prep station for cookies, another it's a homework station, and another it's a place to plop down the laptop and pay bills. Before you know it, the table is a drop zone for paper, books, and pencils. Suddenly, the table surface area is gone, and then you're left to wonder: Where will we go to, ya know, eat?

Keeping your dining room free from nondining clutter encourages everyone to slow down, sit, and enjoy a meal in a relaxed way. And, with the right setup, you can create a warm place to socialize not only during holidays and parties, but also for everyday catch-ups on the days in between. On the flip side, if you're using your dining room only for special occasions, now's the time to revamp your setup and make it work for you every day.

Always have the dining room looking like you're expecting guests at any moment. It'll give joy (and sanity) when it's time for your next meal. (Opposite page) Your table linens don't have to match perfectly, but a coordinated runner and napkins make the whole setup seem clean.

SPRUCE UP YOUR EATING SPACE (NO, NOT YOUR BILLS/HOMEWORK/ SCHOOL PROJECT SPACE) WITH A FEW THOUGHTFUL AND PRACTICAL DETAILS. NOT EVERY BREAKFAST HAS TO BE BRUNCHWORTHY, BUT TAKING EXTRA TIME TO SET UP YOUR DINING ROOM DOES MAKE EVERY MEAL MORE ENJOYABLE.

Keep Some Things on the Table

Your dining room table should be a clean surface, but it doesn't have to be a barren desert of decor. Keep a couple of items—salt and pepper shakers, a trivet, water pitcher, or flowers—in the center of the table to spark visual interest and show personality. Then, make sure the rest of the table is clear.

Remove Anything Not Food-Related

If papers and magazines have started to pile up on the dining room table, purchase folders or boxes to store them, then move it all to the home office or your command center. Now these papers have a new home, and you won't be as tempted to toss them on the table next time. If it's homework that keeps piling up, instruct the little ones to keep loose papers in folders in their backpacks between study sessions, a lesson that will help them well into undergrad.

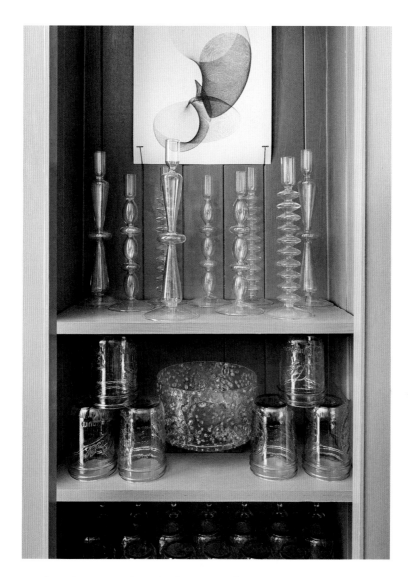

Store China Carefully

Use heavy-duty plastic wrap to cover each plate individually, and stack them, up to eight high, before securing them tightly with the wrap, a trick that caterers use all the time. The dishes won't budge, and they'll be protected from dust so there's no need to wash them before using. Store the stacks in a cupboard, and label them so they're easy to find when the in-laws roll up. As for wineglasses and Champagne flutes, load up commercial-style dishwasher racks, and wrap them in plastic so everything stays safe and clean.

Declutter the China Cabinet

If your wedding china and crystal hasn't seen the light of day since you said, "I do," put it on display in your cabinet or buffet. (You chose it for a reason, so let it see some sunshine!) One or two plates per cabinet windowpane is a good rule of thumb. That way, you're not creating visual clutter. Any overflow can go in storage cases in the cabinets below. If your cabinet overfloweth with glasses and plates, use floating shelves in the same material as your cabinet to add extra space without taking up square footage.

Stash Your Silverware

If you're without a traditional china cabinet, use six-piece place setting rolls for your fancy silverware. The protective cloth prevents silver and silver plate from scratching and tarnishing, and you can fit more in a narrow drawer than you would with a flatware organizer.

Stow the Soft Stuff

Drawers are great places for keeping place mats, runners, tablecloths, linen napkins, and other bulky items. Or, stash them in a bench, which can become extra seating when your dinner-guest number goes up by one person at the last minute.

Keep Table Accessories Close

There's nothing like a candlelit dinner . . . until you realize that candles are the exact kind of where-are-they-when-you-need-them item that you end up rebuying when you can't find them. Keep track of like items with a grid of interlocking drawer inserts tailored to the contents, whether it's plastic silverware for birthday cake or candles for your anniversary. A tiered rolling cart can become a table-setting station. Use it to hold glasses, dishes, and table linens.

4 Ways to Set Your Table

WHETHER IT'S THANKSGIVING OR JUST TUESDAY, HERE'S HOW
TO PUT YOUR PERSONAL STYLE ALL OUT ON THE TABLE.

Modern

Natural elements and layers of texture elevate a neutral color scheme, while warm wooden accents prevent it from seeming stark. If you choose to add in color, keep it simple with just one shade (like aqua or yellow). Create a centerpiece of artfully arranged woodland accents, such as pinecones, faux antlers, and feathers, and finish off each setting with a mini wreath and place card.

Classic

Enhance a simple blue-and-white color scheme with metallic touches, like gilded flatware and gold-rimmed chargers. To keep traditional dinnerware from feeling ultra formal, pair it with more casual items, like fringed napkins and clean-lined, modern glasses. Skip napkin rings and place cards altogether and instead, blanket the table with soft candlelight and milky white blooms (choose anemones with a dark center for drama and contrast).

Preppy

A color scheme of peach, pink, and soft green is a break from traditional holiday colors. Ground your design with a few more saturated items, like a piece of burnt orange pottery and a patterned napkin. Incorporate classic elements with a twist: A whitewashed charger and dip-dyed flatware make the arrangement feel more contemporary. Fairy-tale pumpkins (find them at your local grocery or nursery) make a charming centerpiece; add dusty green eucalyptus and in-season fruits to complete the look.

Organic

Combine burlap, raw wood, and terra-cotta accessories with jewel-toned glassware, cutlery, and linens to create an enchanting garden-inspired tablescape. These items don't all have to match—an eclectic assortment enhances the relaxed, boho feel. Go wild with a runner of greenery and autumnal blooms, and use the leftovers to make flower crowns and boutonnieres for your guests.

Pro Tip

"Treat your china with the same care you took to select it, and display only the items you use to dine: no photo frames, figurines, or other small knickknacks that will clog up the works. And remember, not every china piece was born to be a star, so it's ok to edit what you show off. You can also rotate and curate dishes and platters every few months to keep things fresh."

—JENI ARON, THE CLUTTER COWGIRL

Organize This

TRANSFORM YOUR <u>BAR CART</u> INTO A VERSATILE AND STYLISH SERVING STATION.

LAYER UP

A multilevel cart will give you a place to store pretty crystal and glassware that doesn't get everyday use, like tumblers for whiskey, decanters for wine, and flutes for bubbly.

MAKE IT PRETTY

Other than to hold booze, a bar cart's purpose is to look pretty, so keep your most attractive bottles in the spotlight. The cheap wine and other bottles can be kept in a cabinet in the kitchen out of sight, and mixers should be kept in the fridge.

GET READY TO MINGLE

Whiskey, gin, vodka, a garnish or two, and a snack should do it when it's party time. Only then should you bring out straws and paper or plastic cups. (They can be stored in the china cabinet until then.) That way, guests who have "their drink" can make one themselves.

JUST BE CHILL

When guests come over for a drink, an ice bucket and tongs are hostess lifesavers. (Do you really want to be running to the freezer for ice every time someone needs a drink?) Or, stainless steel ice cubes keep cocktails cold without watering them down.

The Tools

CHINA CABINET OR BUFFET

CLOTH SILVERWARE ROLLS

Rather than working them into your everyday utensil drawers, store your special pieces in a compact roll.

BENCH WITH HIDDEN STORAGE

HANDHELD VACUUM OR WHISK-BROOM SET

A quilted china storage bag is like a cloud for your china. It's super-soft and keeps plates dust-free and in perfect condition until you're ready to whip them out for the holidays.

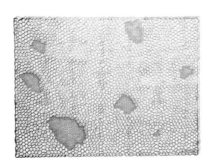

PLACE MATS

TRIVETS

WINE RACK

Store red wine outside the fridge and away from direct sunlight. If wine is left in a room hotter than 70 degrees, the bottle can age too quickly.

VASES

Small-Space Solutions

IF YOU HAVE A DINING ROOM IN YOUR APARTMENT OR SMALL HOME, IT'S PROBABLY NOT SPRAWLING SPACE FOR A LARGE DINNER PARTY. MAKE EVERY INCH COUNT BY USING PIECES THAT DO DOUBLE DUTY WHEN IT'S DINNERTIME.

Drop It

Invest in a drop-leaf table so that when guests come over, you have enough space around the table without it taking up too much acreage the rest of the time. Hang extra folding chairs along a wall or hallway.

Improvise a Table

Maybe you don't even have room for a dining table and chairs. Instead, go with a tiny bar table set against a wall or a mirror, which makes it look bigger, or install a large floating shelf along one wall and put stools under it for a DIY bar setup that's slim and chic.

Think Round

If you've got a corner to spare, tuck a tiny round dining room table there with a hidden storage bench lining the walls as your seating. It will take up less room than a rectangular table, and you can store linens and extra place settings in the bench.

Style Your Shelving

Instead of a bulky buffet, opt for open shelving that keeps the room light and airy. Keep the look uncluttered by buying your dinnerware (plates, bowls, etc.) in the same color and arranging them in neat stacks along the shelves.

Uplift Your Lighting

Wall-mounted lights, like sconces, don't take up any floor room and add a chic look to a small dining space. Add a dimmer to set a mood for entertaining.

The Real Simple Method Checklist

IF YOU HAVE . . .

15 Minutes

☐ **MOVE THOSE PAPERS**. Arrange loose papers into piles, grab the laptop, and move it all off the table. There's no time to go through everything and decide what goes where, so just get it all out of sight by putting papers in a file folder or desk drawer for later.

☐ **ARRANGE THE CHAIRS**. Halfway pulled out chairs look messy. Pushing in chairs and making sure they're the right distance apart from each other give the appearance that you totally have it all together.

☐ **PUT OUT PLACE MATS**. A simple move like arranging place mats around the table makes you look organized in a flash.

1 Hour

☐ **DO A DRAWER OR TWO**. Take inventory in the drawers of your buffet or cabinet and ask yourself if you're using the space efficiently. (If you weren't sure what a drawer was holding before opening it, then you probably aren't.)

A Weekend

☐ **GET AT THAT CHINA**. It's time to take stock of what you have and inspect it for any broken or missing pieces. Lay everything out on the floor or dining room table so you can see everything at once. Make a wish list of things you need, like a gravy boat, and keep only what fits in the cabinet. Just make sure to wash everything before you wrap it up to go inside.

☐ **DO THE SAME WITH LINENS**. Go through your linens and look for stains or yellowing. Send bigger, more precious items off to the dry cleaners. Wash the little things, like napkins and place mats, on your own.

Keep It That Way

Whether your dining room is a place for daily meals or only for Sunday suppers, it's an important space to keep tidy for when it's time to eat. After all, who wants to transfer piles from the dining room table to the kitchen counters or the buffet before chowing down? Here's how to maintain order.

Be Your Own Guest

If you think of yourself as a guest in your own space, you're less likely to let things pile up. You probably wouldn't let mail or unused napkins pile up if you were a guest, right? Bring things that feel unsightly or out of place in the dining room to another part of the house, or return them to their designated place so that you won't be scrambling to get the room in order the next time.

Shine Bright

Make sure you're seeing the results of your hard work in the kitchen by the light of a clean chandelier or lighting fixture. For chandeliers, dust the hardware and the crystals with a dry, lint-free cloth. If the chandelier is extremely dirty, take it apart and individually soak each crystal in rubbing alcohol; then wipe them down. Slip on lint-free gloves (no fingerprints!) and dry each crystal individually with a microfiber cloth. Rehang the crystals. For dome lights and pendants, dust the hardware and the wall-hanging cord with an extendable duster. Spritz a cloth with ammonia-free glass cleaner and wipe the dome gently.

Drop Everything for a Spill

If you let a dinner mess sit, it solidifies and takes up more time (and elbow grease) when you finally do clean it.

Make the Table

It sounds silly to have a fully made table ready at all times, but setting up place mats and plates at your dining room table means you're less likely to make the area your home office where papers can tend to pile up.

Do Some Rug Rehab

Dining room rugs tend to get a lot of traffic, not to mention all that falling food. Vacuum under the table once a week, and once a season, wrap up the whole thing and send it to the dry cleaners.

Edit Your Wares

It can be tempting to pick up adorable pieces from a flea market or to try something from a hot new online potter. But your china cabinet can only hold so much, so stick to a strict one-in, one-out policy when you bring home new plates or serving ware.

THE HACK

Put a small handheld vacuum in the china cabinet for when the snack mix spills. Presto!

IF YOU DO ONE THING EVERY DAY

Take five minutes at the end of each day to clear out items that don't belong. Laptops, homework, and school projects all get the boot back to their proper homes.

Ask the Organizer

Q: If we're not hosting anyone and don't eat there except for fancy meals, why does it matter what's on our dining room table?

A: We often eat on the run, heading to work, school, activities. The importance of an organized dining room is that it encourages everyone to slow down, sit, and enjoy a meal in a relaxed way. A dining room can also be the center of socializing and holidays, so when a dining room is organized, it creates harmony for the focal point of most gatherings—eating.

—JENI ARON, THE CLUTTER COWGIRL

Chapter 5

The Bedroom

YOU'LL SLEEP EASY WITH A SOLID ORGANIZATION PLAN.

YOUR BEDROOM is your sanctuary—and it's also the place where you frantically try on every pair of jeans in your closet before tossing them all aside and deciding on a trusty black skirt as you run out the door. Your bedroom is where you keep some of your most precious items, such as that necklace that's been passed down from your grandmother. And it's the place that holds the one piece of furniture that offers true peace—your bed. But even though your bedroom is meant to be a place of serenity, it can often be where clutter piles up the most.

And, if you share a bedroom with a partner, that can mean double the pileup, so it's important that everything have a designated place (no drawer overflow allowed), and there are systems at work to make sure things stay in those places, from the closet to the bedside tables. That way, neither one of you will have any trouble resting your sweet heads.

A see-through nightstand is a place you can store books and pretty objects without adding too much visual clutter. Stop your stack of books halfway up the space so you leave enough room to breathe. (Opposite page) A floating dresser is a brilliant solution in small spaces because it takes up less room than a traditional one. Tuck a basket of extra pillows or books in the space below.

IF THE BEDROOM IS JUST FOR
SLEEPING, THEN HOW DID YOUR
TENNIS RACKET GET IN HERE?
FIRST, CLEAR OUT YOUR NON-
BEDROOM CLUTTER SO YOU CAN
MAKE SPACE FOR THE THINGS
THAT DO BELONG THERE. YOU'LL
REST EASY WITH THIS SOLID
ORGANIZING PLAN.

Make Your Bed Every Day

You're probably not shocked to be
seeing this one here because it's true.
Making your bed every day declutters
your room instantly, and some research
even suggests that bed-makers get
better sleep than those who don't. Do
it as soon as you wake up so you won't
be dreading it later. Even if laundry
and stacks of books are piling up
around you, a made bed clears your
mind—and might even inspire you to
tackle that laundry.

Buy a Bed with Storage

There are a few ways to find extra
storage room in your bed. If books
and magazines keep piling up around
you, hide them in a headboard that
doubles as a bookshelf for all your
paged treasures. Similarly, lots of beds
have built-in, under-the-bed drawers
for storing extra sets of sheets or bulky
clothing. Some even have mattresses
that lift up so you can store off-season
clothing or bedding underneath.

Measure Your Bedside Tables

To keep the space next to the bed looking clean, choose nightstands that are the height of the bed or an inch or two lower. In general, a height of 24 to 27 inches looks best. If you want to try a mismatched pair of tables, make sure both are the same height or within two inches of each other. A surface that's at least 18 inches deep allows you to fit a lamp plus an object or two, like a clock, stack of books, or vase.

Pick the Right-Sized Reading Lamp

Rather than lighting up things with a wide shade, go for a sleek desk lamp that takes up less space, is flexible, and is the right size for reading in bed. The light should be 13 to 15 inches above the surface of the mattress to give you the best light.

Maximize Your Dresser

First, clear off the surface. Stash the odd items that normally clutter up the dresser landscape—sunglasses, occasional jewelry, nail polish, receipts, lotions—into a place-for-everything drawer divider tucked into a top drawer. When it comes to the rest of the drawers, start by giving each one a clear category (undergarments, shirts, bottoms). To create more room, move off-season items, like swimsuits or heavy sweaters, to a bin on a top shelf of a closet or some other out-of-the-way spot, like under the bed. It's helpful to give the remaining pieces in the drawers some structure: Use dividers to segment socks, underwear, and bras. For T-shirts, consider this: You can fit about a third more T-shirts in a drawer by folding and rolling them and then filing them vertically. The best part is that this method keeps logos, patterns, or labels displayed, making it a cinch for you to hunt down the top you desperately need on a given day. And, if you're unsure how to best split a drawer, default to equal quadrants. Then, sort by style or color, whichever makes it easier to spot that one pair of undies you need for those white jeans. If drawer space is still tight, try transferring other items to the closet (T-shirts and jeans, folded on shelves; workout clothes, grouped together in a bin).

Free Up the Bedroom Chair for— Gasp—Sitting

Bottomless mounds of discarded jeans and tops on that seat make your bedroom a stressful spot. To give you a place to sit, put a freestanding valet behind the buried chair or in a corner of the room so you can neatly hang garments there instead. Or, make a rule that you're not allowed to get into bed at night without clearing off the chair first.

Three Apps to Boost Bedroom Comfort

1

White Noise

Light sleepers who want to muffle things that go bump in the night can choose from 40-plus soothing sounds, like rain, fan, and grandfather clock. Or record your own (waves at the beach, say) to play on a loop. **(99 cents, iTunes)**

2

Sleep Cycle

This "intelligent alarm clock" uses your smartphone's accelerometer to monitor your movements all night so it can wake you up during your light sleep phase, leaving you refreshed, not groggy. **(free, iTunes)**

3

F.Lux

At night, this app dims the sleep-disrupting blue light of a screen automatically, allowing you to surf the web before you turn in without disturbing your circadian rhythms. **(free, justgetflux.com)**

Make Space for Bedding Overflow

Decorative pillows are great for, well, decoration, but when it comes to actually sleeping, sometimes you need to move them aside. Designate a spot in your room to store them when you're actually getting shuteye—it could be under a floating nightstand, or on a bench at the end of the bed. Just make sure that you put all the pillows back in their pretty place on the bed once you've made it in the AM. You're a person who makes the bed every day now, remember?

Organize This

GIVE YOUR OUT-OF-CONTROL <u>UNDIE DRAWER</u> A MAKEOVER.

LEAVE SOME SPACE

Reserve room for love notes or other keepsakes that make you smile when getting dressed—plus a packet of fashion tape to grab on the go.

STASH YOUR SUNDRIES

Little bottles of lingerie cleaner and spray for delicates get lost in the laundry room; tuck them here to make it easier (and more motivating) to do your hand washables.

ADD A POP OF PATTERN

Pretty drawer liners are a visual cue to keep items neat and treat this spot like a special space.

SORT IT OUT

Divide your underthings by category and color. The morning rush is less insane when this drawer feels like a boutique rather than a bargain bin.

MAKE A MODULAR MIX

Collapsible, movable organizers structure this open space, giving you an easy system to corral unmentionables (shapewear in one, sports bras in another).

The Closet

WELCOME TO TOTAL
CLOSET BLISS.

Try a Closet Time-saver

Starting now, whenever you take out an article of clothing, put the empty hanger back at one end of the rod (the same end each time). Collecting them all in one spot keeps clothes neat and means never having to hunt for a hanger again. Avoid a chaotic jumble of wire, wood, and plastic hangers by choosing just one type and brand of hanger (slim velvet ones give you the most space) for your closet.

Double Your Closet Space

Attach a trapeze-style second rod to your existing rod to store pants below tops instead of squishing them in all together. For a standard-size closet, choose one that's three feet wide to leave room for hanging dresses on the side.

Think Creatively

You don't have to hang everything that's in your closet. Use hanging shelves and wire racks to organize folded shirts, sweaters, and jeans by color and weight. Purses or hats (like fedoras) also rest well on hanging shelves where they won't get smashed.

Store Shoes Where You Can See Them

Make sure all of your footwear is on display—otherwise, you'll never wear what you can't see. A space saver: Add inserts to boots to prevent toppling. For more special pairs of shoes, buy shoe boxes with windows or clear plastic boxes so you can see what's inside. That said, it's also a good idea to switch your stash every season so bulky snow boots don't take up sandal space in the summer. If you are tight on space, try flipping one shoe in each pair so they sit toe to heel.

Show Off Your Jewelry

House your baubles in a roomy piece of furniture that allows you to keep everything spread out in single layers rather than clumps. Try a tall, skinny lingerie chest, and equip the drawers with flocked divided trays. Limit each drawer to a single jewelry type—bracelets in one, earrings in another. If you want to give some favorites a prominent spot, hang them on hooks in your closet. Prefer to keep all the jewelry out in the open? Pin each piece to a fabric-covered memo board mounted on the wall.

Set Boundaries for Handbags

Install shelf dividers to keep purses upright and to eliminate pileups. If you can't fit all your bags in that space, consider it your cue to downsize. And, you know those dust bags that come with purses? Don't hide your bag inside of them, or you won't be able to see your collection. Instead, use the dust bag to fill the purse when it's not in use, which will help it stand up and keep its shape.

Embrace the Clear Plastic Box

A clear shoebox can also double as a place to stash silk scarves, rolled belts, and other small items like neckties and pocket squares so that they're always visible. Then, stack them with the shoes. Voilà!

Make Space for Out-of-Season Clothes

Add an armoire or trunk to your bedroom to store off-season stuff, like sweaters or sundresses. Just make sure the clothes are clean before storing them. If you're transitioning into summer, store cashmere sweaters in large zippered plastic bags, and stick them in the freezer for a few hours to kill off any bug larvae. Then store them in a breathable cotton garment box under a bed or on a shelf. For hanging items, swap foam-strip, dry-cleaner hangers for wood, plastic, or padded ones, because the foam can discolor a favorite shirt. The same applies to hangers flocked in a dark, velvet-like material—they can transfer color to garments over time.

Presort Laundry

Presort your linens with a three-part hamper that has a bin for lights, darks, and colors. This will help make laundry day less of a chore. Finding one on wheels makes it easy to transport it from closet to laundry room in a cinch. And, if the canvas bags need refreshing, toss them into the machine as well.

LAYOUT WISDOM

A smart closet addresses four key areas: hanging clothes, folded pieces, shoes, and accessories. There's no one way to arrange your space, but to determine the setup that will work best for you, be realistic about the square footage you have and work within these guidelines.

DOORS

Hinged full-swing or bifold doors give full access, whereas dual-hung sliding doors prevent access to the center. If every inch counts, consider replacing sliding doors with hinged ones or doors that slide all the way open on a rail.

CLOTHING RODS

If your closet ceiling height is at least 7½ feet, you have room for two rods (one hung about three or four feet above the other), which can maximize space. A clothing rod should hang at least 42 inches above the floor so that clothes don't drag. Position the rod at least a foot from the back wall, if possible. There should be at least 3 inches beyond the ends of your hangers.

The low rod can hold skirts and pants; an eye-level pole can hold dresses and tops. If you can, leave breathing room between garments—at least ¼ inch, if possible, with fabrics barely grazing one another. Again, seasonality and frequency of use can be a big factor in delegating space: That taffeta evening gown in the roomy garment bag may have to be stored somewhere else.

MAKE SURE YOU MEASURE YOUR SPACE PRECISELY (TO THE NEAREST SIXTEENTH OF AN INCH) BEFORE BUYING RODS, SHELVING UNITS, OR OTHER HARDWARE.

SHELVES

Leave some space in your closet for shelves, which are crucial for holding sweaters and delicate knits (or any clothing that will stretch out of shape on a hanger), accessories (totes, purses), storage boxes, and shoes. Shelves should be open and not deeper than 14 inches; otherwise, you'll have to hunt around for what should be close at hand. Wooden shelves are sturdy and nice-looking. Metal and plastic-coated wire shelving units are solid options too, but those can potentially "rib" clothing. Acids in wooden shelves, including cedar, can deteriorate fabric, so line them with shelf paper or unbleached, undyed washed muslin (sold at fabric stores). If you don't want to buy expensive custom shelving or are tight on space, consider adding hanging shelves.

DRAWERS

Whether they're mounted to the closet wall or part of a chest positioned inside the closet, drawers help you organize small pieces, like undergarments and accessories. If installing drawers is too costly or complicated, substitute baskets placed on shelves.

A CLEAN-SWEEP CHECKLIST

☐ Empty your closet of the past season's clothes, stashing rarely worn pieces in a box for charity.

☐ Wipe down the closet with a mild, fresh-smelling soap.

☐ Wash or dry-clean your clothes (insects and moths are attracted to dirt, not the clothing).

☐ Repair any tears, and replace buttons.

"I personally organize my closet by type, and then within each type, I organize by color. So, for example, in the area where I hang my dresses, my dresses are organized by color, which makes it easier for me to find pieces when I am looking for a specific item, like when I think, 'I feel like wearing a red dress tonight!'"

—ALEXANDRA WILSON,
COFOUNDER OF FITZ, A CLOSET-STYLING COMPANY

Organize This

FORGET FISHING FOR YOUR KEYS
BY EDITING DOWN YOUR HANDBAG.

CORD CORRALLER

Bundle wires in this genius little piece of leather and you'll never again face that annoying task of detangling earbuds or cables from your umbrella.

EYE-CATCHING KEY CHAIN

A holder that's a substantial size keeps keys from getting buried in the bottom of your bag.

PORTABLE POUCH

Stash makeup and jewelry in a lined, dual-compartment case for quick, no-thinking-required bag swaps when racing from the gym to the office to an evening out.

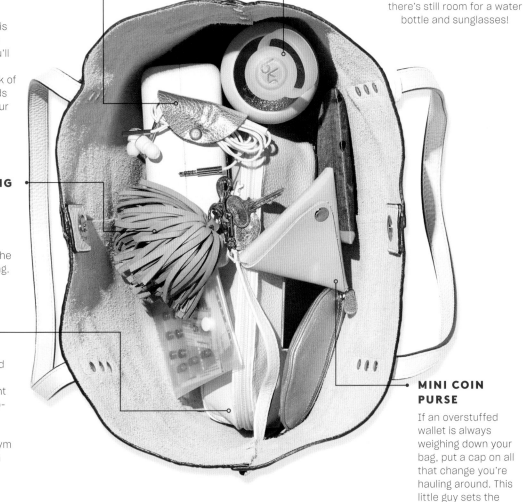

All this stuff in here, and there's still room for a water bottle and sunglasses!

MINI COIN PURSE

If an overstuffed wallet is always weighing down your bag, put a cap on all that change you're hauling around. This little guy sets the limit for you.

PARE DOWN YOUR PURSE

Tuck a clean, empty plastic sandwich bag into your handbag. When you find yourself with a chunk of idle time—waiting in a doctor's office, stuck on a long phone call—fill it up with nonessentials to trash or relocate later.

The Tools

BED WITH STORAGE

SHELF DIVIDERS

NIGHTSTANDS

CLEAR BINS

FOLDING BOARD

Use a folding board to create
uniform shirt stacks; then "file"
them vertically into your dresser.

Ask almost any organizer and they'll tell you: velvet slimline hangers are the most efficient way to fit everything—from suits to dresses to jeans—in your closet. We're partial to these Real Simple ones (wink, wink).

SHOE ORGANIZER

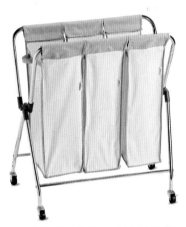

THREE-PART HAMPER

SHOE BOXES WITH A VIEW

UNDER-THE-BED STORAGE

Small-Space Solutions

IN A BEDROOM THAT'S ACTUALLY MORE BED THAN
ROOM, IT'S IMPORTANT TO WISELY DIVVY UP THE SPACE
YOU HAVE LEFT BY CHOOSING MULTIPURPOSE FURNITURE
AND ARRANGING IT IN THE MOST EFFICIENT WAY.

Lift the Bed

Bed raisers are a genius way
to give yourself more storage
room underneath for larger
items like suitcases and
file boxes.

Mount Your Lights and Nightstand

Opt for space-saving wall lamps
or sconces. A floating nightstand
or shelf visually elongates your
space while creating an open
area underneath to stash slippers.

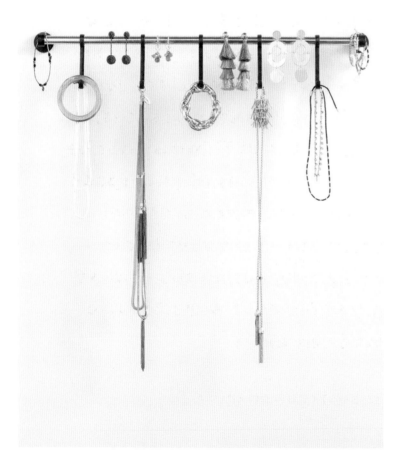

Make Furniture Multitask

Who says a desk can only be a desk?
Assign it the role of nightstand and
vanity when it's arranged next to
your bed. Or, if your space is even
too tiny for a workspace, a breakfast
tray with folding legs can hold a
laptop when you're sitting up in bed
and can be neatly stashed under the
bed when it's lights out.

Display Your Baubles

Hang a slim rod or small corkboard
on a closet wall, and display
necklaces and earrings so you can
see everything and grab what you
need in a flash.

Put the Windowsill to Work

In a super-tight space, push the
head of your bed up against
the windowsill as a makeshift
"headboard." You can store
reading materials and a plant or
two there.

Go For Light Colors

White and creams can make a small
space appear larger, lighter, and less
cluttered. Plus, that often means no
painting when you move in or out.

Q: Shoes, shoes, shoes. They're littering the floor of my closet. Help!

A: The way you store your shoes depends on the layout of your closet, but the first rule is that you should be able to see them all. (And not because they're scattered on the floor.) Make a system that consists of visible shelving, as well as pretty boxes with windows reserved for your "most special" shoes. If you can see the shoes, you're more likely to wear them. This may not be possible depending on the realities of your space and how many shoes you own, so do seasonal switch outs. You don't need to see your boots in the summer, and similarly, during the coldest months of the year, you may not want to have your sandals front and center.

—ALEXANDRA WILSON,
COFOUNDER OF FITZ, A CLOSET-STYLING COMPANY

The Real Simple Method Checklist

IF YOU HAVE . . .

15 Minutes

☐ **MAKE YOUR BED.** In just one minute, you've decluttered the biggest piece of furniture in the room.

☐ **CLOSE THE CLOSET DOORS.** If you can't see the chaos behind them, it's like it doesn't exist, right? In any case, it's a quick fix that really works.

1 Hour

☐ **CLEAR OFF THE DRESSER.** Toss receipts and papers you don't need, and put jewelry and beauty products back in their proper places. Create as much open surface space as possible—one stack of books or a few objects you enjoy is enough.

☐ **PUT AWAY PILES OF CLOTHES.** Toss dirty items into the hamper, and hang up or fold anything else. Set aside dry cleaning for your next trip. Ahhh, there's that bedroom chair again!

☐ **TIDY UP THE NIGHTSTANDS.** Put books into neat stacks, and move water glasses or coffee mugs back to the kitchen where they belong.

☐ **DESIGNATE YOUR DRESSER DRAWERS.** Make sure each drawer is organized by the type of clothing it contains, and place drawer dividers accordingly. Refold everything that's going inside (even pants) so that they now sit vertically, and you can see everything that's in the drawer.

☐ **REPLACE OLD PILLOWS.** When your head cushions start to lose shape permanently, it's time to buy new ones. Or, refresh the old ones with a spritz from a spray bottle filled with vodka, which sanitizes, every time you change your sheets.

A Weekend

☐ **OVERHAUL YOUR CLOSET.** Even if it's not time to switch seasons, it's probably time for a refresh. Remove everything from the shelves and rods so you can see what's been hiding in there all these months. Divide clothing, shoes, and bags into three categories: Keep, Toss, Donate. Then put everything back according to your new decided-upon organizing system. Anything that doesn't fit in the closet goes in a dresser drawer, assuming there's room there, or goes in the Toss or Donate pile.

Keep It That Way

Mornings are usually not the time most of us want to be delicately folding sweaters and placing them back in drawers while searching for the right one. Here's how to stick to a plan you can follow no matter how frantic your day gets.

Take Stock of your Closet

Every two months, take an hour or two to tidy up and edit out pieces that you no longer need; then donate them, or resell the good stuff. Also, organized people trick themselves with treats. Attach a reward to a tedious task: Tell yourself that you can get a pedicure after you've organized your closet or that you can watch a movie after you've sorted your underwear drawer. You'll actually follow through.

Stay Strong

More than any other room of the house, your bedroom is the most important one to follow the one-in, one-out rule. After all, there aren't many places where a pair of jeans can go when they don't fit in a drawer or have a hanger—and remember, that chair is not an option. Take that attitude with you when you're shopping to avoid buying doubles. If you can't remember if you already have a v-neck black sheath, closet inventory website and app Finery (finery.com) is like the computerized Clueless closet. It searches your past purchases and lets you upload images to help you create a virtual closet and keep track of what you want to purchase in the future.

THE HACK

You know those hanging fruit baskets that we mentioned earlier in the kitchen chapter? They're also great for storing scarves, knit hats, and gloves. In the summer, swap in your bathing suits and cover-ups.

IF YOU DO ONE THING EVERY DAY

You probably know what we're going to say here, right? Make your bed. Yep, it's the easiest way to feel put together in the AM, and some research has shown that people who make their beds are happier than those who let the sheets lie where they may.

HOW OFTEN SHOULD I WASH MY...?

SHEETS AND PILLOWCASES
Every week

DUVET COVER
Every two weeks

COMFORTER
If it's covered by a duvet, never! (Unless it gets wet.)

QUILT
Dry-clean twice a year

PILLOWS
Every six months. Spritz with vodka in between.

Take Care Of Your Mattress

Yes, it is possible to wash—well, freshen and deodorize—a mattress. Every six months, remove and launder the cover, and sprinkle the mattress with baking soda until the top has a thin coating on it. Let the baking soda sit for five to ten minutes, then vacuum it off using the upholstery attachment of a vacuum cleaner.

Take Off Your Shoes in Your Closet

Tell yourself that you can't start dinner (or watch *This is Us*) until you make it to your closet so that they go back into their correct bin, pocket, or shelf. If your shoes started the day in the bedroom closet, make sure to return them there as soon as you step in the door.

Light It Up

You're more likely to keep everything in its place if you can see what you're working with. Inexpensive, battery-operated motion-sensor lights turn on when you walk in the closet and turn off 30 seconds later. Mount them to the ceiling or on the side wall.

Chapter 6

The Bathroom

KEEP YOUR WASHING SPACE SO FRESH AND SO CLEAN.

FOR A ROOM that has so much traffic and holds so many things—from razors to electric toothbrushes (and their chargers) to toilet paper—it's kind of shocking how little storage space most bathrooms have. That means you often have to edit and think creatively about where to put those extra toothbrush heads. The medicine cabinet is a good place to start. By using that space efficiently, you'll make mornings and evenings that much smoother. But there are plenty of other ways to cleverly use what little bathroom space you have.

Because the bathroom is a space that everyone in the family visits every day, multiple times a day, it's important that everything has a place, and that everyone knows where that place is, especially when the toilet paper runs out. And, remember: It's not one person's job to keep the bathroom tidy on a daily basis, so pick a plan that everyone can understand and stick to—no matter how hectic your mornings or bedtimes might be. Your daily routines are about to get a whole lot smoother.

A storage unit with shelves gives you a place for towels and other bath accessories, especially in a tight space. (Opposite page) Hide a built-in hamper inside your bathroom counter cabinets, and designate it for towels only. That way you won't have to do any sorting on laundry day.

IT'S TRUE THAT THIS HIGH-TRAFFIC AREA REQUIRES ALMOST CONSTANT EFFORT TO STAY SPOTLESS. BUT THERE IS GOOD NEWS: SETTLING INTO A SOLID ARRANGEMENT HELPS KEEP THE SPACE CLUTTER-FREE, NO MATTER HOW MANY (OR HOW FEW!) FAMILY MEMBERS SHARE IT.

Use Counter Space to Your Advantage

Keep only things on the counter that you use every day, like toothbrushes and hand soap. Other small items, like cotton swabs, can go on a small tray, if necessary. That should leave plenty of surface area for when it's time to take out your blow-dryer or makeup, or when men need to get out their shaving gear.

Toss Your Tired Products

Even ruthless purgers tend to hold on to lotion and potions for too long. But all items become less effective over time. Throw out anything that smells or looks funny or that you know is well past its prime. Many products have a "period after opening" label, a number followed by the letter M. It indicates how many months the item is effective after opening.

Show Your Disposables

So you can see when supplies are dwindling and know when it's time to stock up, put everyday essentials, including cotton balls and swabs, in clear containers. Consider using any repurposed vessels or apothecary jars. Keep makeup brushes upright and accessible in a tumbler to avoid dusting up your drawers or damaging the bristles.

Keep Makeup Visible

Only place products you use daily on the counter. Gather items into small containers or in a multitiered rotating organizer so they don't take over the entire space. If a container overflows, it's time for a quick purge. The rest is better off in a secondary space, like under the sink or in a drawer. Sort like with like, and keep the products visible in clear containers or in a drawer organizer. (When buying drawer organizers, select small boxes over large units to make it easier to customize to your needs, whether you have five lipsticks or 50.) Tight on space? Store brushes and eyeliner pencils in magnetic organizers inside the medicine cabinet door.

How Often Do I Really Need to Replace That?

For an easy way to track how long you've had a product, write the month and year when you first open it on a small sticker or piece of masking tape, and affix it to the bottom of the jar or tube.

ITEM	HOW LONG IT LASTS
Bar soap	18 months to 3 years
Bath oil	1 year
Body bleaches and depilatories	6 months
Body lotion	2 years
Body wash	3 years
Concealer	1 year
Cream blush	1 year
Deodorant	1 to 2 years
Disposable razors	every 5-7 shaves
Eye cream	1 year
Eye liner	3 months
Eye liner pencil	2 years
Eye shadow	1 year
Face cream	2 years
Foundation	1 year
Hairbrush	1 year
Hair gel	2 to 3 years
Hair spray	2 to 3 years
Lip balm	1 to 5 years
Lip gloss	1 year
Lipstick	2 years
Liquid eyeliner	3 months
Loofah	6 months
Makeup sponge	1 month
Mascara	3 months
Medications	check your labels
Mouthwash	3 years from manufacture date
Nail polish	1 year
Nail polish remover	indefinitely
Perfume	1 to 2 years
Powder blush	2 years
Shampoo and conditioner	2 to 3 years
Shaving cream	2 years
Sunscreen	3 years
Toothbrush	3 months
Tooth-whitening strips	13 months

GOT PRODUCT OVERFLOW? DONATE EXTRA TOILETRIES (LIKE HOTEL MINIS, TOOTHBRUSHES, AND FEMININE-CARE PRODUCTS) TO A NEARBY HOMELESS SHELTER. THESE ITEMS ARE ALMOST ALWAYS IN NEED.

Makeup Brush Cleaning 101

Most experts agree that once a month is fine. Just dip the brush in warm, soapy water—use shampoo or a mild bar soap. Rinse it, blot the brush with a clean towel, then use a blow-dryer to dry the bristles gently.

Always point your brushes downward when washing and never allow a wet brush to dry standing up, as the water will run into the ferrule—the metal band that attaches the bristles to the handle—and loosen the glue that holds the brush and bristles together.

For quick cleansing between washings, you can also use makeup-removing wipes or an antimicrobial microfiber cloth to wipe your brushes and remove residue.

When your brushes aren't in use, store them in a closed container or medicine cabinet to prevent dust and dirt from landing on the bristles, and eventually, your skin.

To clean a foundation sponge or blender, rinse it under warm water, then rub it between your soapy hands and rinse again until the water runs clear. Let it airdry overnight.

Supply Yourself

Daily skin-care essentials are best stored in the medicine cabinet for easy access at the sink and mirror. Stow the items you use only on an as-needed basis—summer sunblock, tampons, guest soaps—in a closet or a closed cabinet. To save money and cut down on waste and trips to the store, buy shampoo, conditioner, and body wash in bulk, and store them here. Decant the products into smaller bottles for the shower and even tinier ones for traveling.

Structure the Under-the-Sink Space

That area under a kitchen or bathroom sink is typically a jumbled mess because of the awkward pipes. The fix: Install a two-tier pullout shelf or a triangular corner shelf that fits around the pipes to turn the area into a tidier one for cleaning products, cloths, sponges, and more. Give medicine cabinet duplicates and lesser-used products, like bath oil and face scrubs, designated space in: canvas bins under the bathroom sink or in the linen closet. Add pizzazz with a nonadhesive shelf paper. (Avoid stick-on papers; glue plus humidity can attract pests.) It will also eliminate scrubbing hard-to-reach nooks. When gunk accumulates, just swap in a fresh sheet.

Take Cover

If you have a pedestal sink that's not pretty enough to be, um, put on a pedestal, make a no-sew fabric skirt. Start with a bedsheet, using the finished hem for the bottom of the skirt. Trim the needed length and width, and "hem" the edges with iron-on hem tape. Affix industrial-strength Velcro (sold at the hardware store) to the top of the skirt and the bottom of the sink, and then attach the skirt. Along with adding some grace to your space, you'll create more coveted hidden storage. The best thing to keep under there is an organizing unit on wheels, like a tiered cart. Roll it out from under the sink to reach extra hand towels and cleaning supplies, then roll it back into hiding when you're finished.

Blankets

Sheets

Towels

Towels

Hand Towels

Bath Towels

Put Up Some Hooks

Tons of towels can take up lots of space. To keep them all neat and dry, hang two or three rows of hooks on the back of the bathroom door. Lower hooks can be for the kids' robes, and parents get the top ones for towels.

Consider the Ceiling

If your quarters are tight and space is already compromised, look up. Take advantage of vertical real estate by hanging a multitier basket for additional storage. When placed in the shower, the open rungs of a three-tier hanging basket allow loofahs and bath toys to dry over the tub. Or suspend the basket in an unused corner and stock it with lotions, treatments, and scented sachets.

Organize Your Bathroom and Linen Closet

Stash towels at eye level, since you'll be reaching for them frequently. Hand towels and washcloths can be rolled and stowed in baskets to prevent toppling stacks.

Create a Primp Kit

Hair dryers, curling irons, brushes, and styling products can become an unruly mess to manage. To keep yours neat, store them in a caddy with many compartments. Take it out when you're doing your hair, then stash the whole kit and caboodle under a sink or in a closet when you're done. Wrap the cords of your curling iron and blow-dryer loosely, like lassos, to maintain their life.

Add Shower Storage

Pick a caddy with just enough space for the necessities. Impose a one-product per purpose policy and apply the limit to everyone. Sturdy plastic containers mounted with strong waterproof adhesive strips stay put. Or, a tension-rod shower tower makes even more room for families who can't agree on the same brand of anything.

"I cannot even begin to tell you how many of my clients keep excessive hotel mini products that never get used and take up valuable space in their bathroom. If you are a person who likes to camp, or someone who uses mini toiletries frequently, then, yes, you have my permission to keep some on stock for planned trips in the near future. However, if you are someone who travels to hotels frequently, then you will have a new, shiny set of hotel minis at the next hotel you visit, and there is absolutely no valid reason for collecting these!"

—LAYNE BROOKSHIRE, ORGANIZER AND FOUNDER OF MS. PLACED

Organize This

MAKE YOUR <u>MEDICINE CABINET</u> ALL BETTER.

SAVE THE TOP SHELF

Use the top shelf for sharp tools (razors, tweezers) and first-aid staples, like antibiotic ointment.

MAXIMIZE STORAGE

Readjust the shelves if you need more height. The middle shelf can hold once-a-day (or every-other-day) items: deodorant, hair gel, shaving cream, and lotions.

MAGNETIZE THE LITTLE THINGS

Tired of losing bobby pins, tweezers, and nail scissors in the back of a drawer or the bottom of a toiletry bag? Attach them to a magnetic strip adhered to the inside of the medicine cabinet door.

GO VERTICAL

Group these usually fallen soldiers (lip balm, sunscreen) in clear canisters to keep them upright and to save space.

FRONT AND CENTER

The bottom shelf is easiest to access, so that's where products you typically use twice a day (or more) should go. It's helpful to group the ones you use together: toothpaste next to mouthwash, saline next to contacts case.

The Tools

TOOTHBRUSH HOLDER

SOAP DISPENSER

SMALL TRAY

TOWEL RACK AND DOOR HOOKS

CLEAR CANISTERS

Seeing just how many cotton balls or pads you have left will let you know when it's time to restock.

UNDER-THE-SINK STORAGE

SHOWER CADDY

CABINET ORGANIZER

Long and shallow drawer organizers are clutch for keeping a medicine cabinet sane. Products won't topple, and you'll have a sense of what fits (and when you need to cut back).

As utilitarian as it is stylish, a ladder towel rack adds vertical storage and a spa-like touch while preserving precious floor real estate. Use it to hang hand towels, reading materials, or wire baskets right on the rungs.

Small-Space Solutions

THERE ARE SO MANY ITTY-BITTY THINGS THAT GO IN A BATHROOM THAT WHEN SPACE IS LIMITED, IT'S TIME TO GET CREATIVE WITH WAYS TO STORE IT ALL.

Make Some Extra Shelf Space

If your medicine cabinet situation is weak, add a shelf right above your sink to hold the things you use every day, like your glasses or face wash. A shelf above the toilet can be a storage spot for extra TP rolls and hand towels.

Take Shape

An oval mirror seems to stretch upwards, making even the teeniest of bathrooms appear slightly larger. Or, a full-length mirror can be a double whammy if you find one with hidden storage behind it—a secret place to stash extra toiletries.

Stretch Out Your Shower

Instead of cramming your tub ledge with shampoo bottles, place a second shower curtain rod near the wall, and add S-hooks to hang small caddies and loofahs so they're out of the way.

Be a Basket Case

Big baskets can act as a surrogate cabinet. To store things that aren't pretty enough to be seen, screw decorative wicker baskets into the wall and toss extra items in there.

The Real Simple Method Checklist

IF YOU HAVE . . .

15 Minutes

☐ **CLEAR OFF THE COUNTERS.** Put loose toothbrushes and products in the medicine cabinet, close the door, and say a little prayer that no one snoops around and opens the cabinet when they come over.

☐ **WIPE DOWN SURFACES.** In a pinch, glass cleaner will give your sink and knobs a sparkly sheen. Then, use it on the mirrors. Ahhh, instant clean.

1 Hour

☐ **PURGE YOUR PRODUCTS.** Scan the shower for empty bottles, and replace them with new products. If you're out, add it to the shopping list.

☐ **REPLACE COTTON BALLS.** Replenish your stash of cotton swabs and balls in their clear canisters.

☐ **FOLD TOWELS.** It takes only a few minutes to make the hanging towels look fresh again in a neat stack. Big towels go on the bottom, and put the smaller hand towels on top.

A Weekend

☐ **MAKE OVER THE MEDICINE CABINET.** Take everything out, and put old or expired products in the trash. Clean the shelves and adjust them so even your tallest products will fit. Then, fill it from the bottom up, placing the things you use most (toothbrushes and face wash) on the bottom shelf, and the products you use the least (medicine and nail polish) on the top shelf.

☐ **ADJUST YOUR IN-SHOWER EXPERIENCE.** Edit the amount of shampoo bottles and body washes by consolidating the family favorites into one, or install caddies to fit everyone's preferences.

☐ **CLEAR OUT UNDER THE SINK.** Take everything out from underneath the sink, and do an inventory, taking your time to see what you use and what you don't. If you don't have an organization system already in place, install a pull-out basket or a corner shelf unit that will bypass the drain pipe. Stock it as needed.

Ask The Organizer

Q: We seem to always be collecting extra toothbrushes. Should we keep or toss?

A: We all have a collection of toothbrushes we actually use and then those that come from the dentist. If you are not likely to use the dentist toothbrush, keep a few on hand for guests that might forget one, and send the rest to the shelter to be donated. Limit the number of places you would find the toothbrush stash by corralling them from everyone in the house and choosing one place for them to live as the extra stock. You can do this with mouthwash, toothpaste, floss, and any regularly used and replenished items.

—LAYNE BROOKSHIRE, ORGANIZER AND FOUNDER OF MS. PLACED

Keep It That Way

In the blink of one hurried morning or evening, the bathroom can become a complete disaster zone. Here's how to maintain your systems—and a cool head—even on the most stressful of days.

Make Small Daily Efforts

Keeping the bathroom tidy each day is a practice, not a miracle. Remind everyone in the family that disorganization can start a chain reaction: They're only slowing down the next person by not putting things back where they belong. Sure, sometimes life gets crazy and you might need to leave the house in a hurry without putting your toothbrush back properly, and that's okay. Because when you've already created homes for where everything should live, it makes cleanup at a later time a cinch.

The Fastest Way To Clean the Bathroom

This is your ultimate once-a-week routine. Afterwards, reward your hard work with—what else?—a hot bath.

1

Clear all bathroom surfaces, removing all toiletries and accessories from the countertop, the tub ledge, and the toilet tank. Put away items that don't belong, and set the rest in a bin on the floor outside the bathroom. Toss used towels directly into the washing machine.

2

Liberally spray the tub, tiles, and the sink basin with an all-purpose disinfecting cleaner. Spritz the toilet exterior and the walls behind and beside it. (With each flush, particles can be launched out of the bowl up to three feet.) Spray the inside of the lid, the top and underside of the seat, and the rim of the bowl. Let the cleaner sit on all surfaces for 5 to 10 minutes. Squirt a ring of toilet-bowl cleaner under the rim of the bowl and let sit.

3

Dust upper areas (light fixtures, fan vents, cabinets, the tops of the door and window frames) with a telescoping microfiber duster. Spray the mirror with glass cleaner and, using a thin (not terry-style) microfiber cloth for glass and polishing, wipe in a tight S-pattern from top to bottom. (This is more effective than a circular motion, which actually redeposits dirt, leaving streaks.) If you're cleaning more than one bathroom, complete the first three steps in each before moving to step 4.

4

Clean midrange and lower spots with a microfiber cloth lightly misted with all-purpose cleaner, working around the room in a circle: towel bars, windowsills, toilet paper holder, and baseboards.

5

Spray countertops with all-purpose disinfecting cleaner, and wipe dry with a clean microfiber cloth. Give anything that lives on the counter (soap dispenser, cotton-swab container, etc.) a quick swipe with the same cloth, and place items back on the counter.

6

Scrub the sink, paying special attention to the drain area. (Use the same cloth you used on the counter.) Rinse, then buff dry. Wipe the faucet and the handles with a fresh cloth.

7

Deal with the trash can. Empty it and, if you don't use a liner, spritz the interior with all-purpose disinfecting cleaner. Let sit for a few minutes, then wipe with a paper towel.

8

Handle the serious stuff. Using paper towels, wipe down all the pretreated parts of the toilet in this order: handle, tank lid, front of tank, top of toilet lid, inside of lid, top and underside of seat, rim of bowl, outside of bowl, toilet base, and around the back. Swap in a new paper towel as needed, and use an old, clean toothbrush to scrub out stubborn grime in nooks and crannies.

IF YOU DO ONE THING EVERY DAY

Wipe down the sink hardware. A sparkling faucet has the magical ability to make the rest of the bathroom appear bright and clean, too.

9

Clean inside the bowl. With the seat up, scrub the bowl with a toilet brush. Flush, then rinse the brush as new water flows in. Close the seat on top of the brush handle so it can drip-dry into the bowl (about 10 minutes or until dry) before setting the brush back in its holder.

10

Dry the pre-treated walls surrounding the toilet with a paper towel. Then, with a dual-sided, nonscratching, scrubbing sponge, wipe down the shower walls and the tub, using the scouring side as needed. (For glass doors, use only a soft kitchen sponge.) Rinse with hot water. If you don't have a handheld showerhead, you can douse the area using a small bucket or a plastic container.

11

Squeegee the shower area to dry it completely. A fan can help get rid of moisture, but a squeegee is the most effective tool.

12

Vacuum to remove any hair or dust on the floor, then mop using all-purpose disinfecting cleaner. Start at the farthest corner from the door and work your way toward the entry. If hard-to-reach spots, like behind the toilet or under the vanity, are too narrow for the mop, get down on your hands and knees (just for a minute!) and use a microfiber cloth with cleaner to sanitize the area.

13

You're done!

THE HACK

For brilliant results minus the elbow grease, rub a dampened dryer sheet over a wet shower door to banish soap-scum buildup.

Chapter 7

The Home Office

TRANSFORM YOUR WORKING SPACE INTO A SPACE THAT WORKS FOR YOU.

IF YOUR KITCHEN is considered the heart of your home, then your home office is the brain. It's where you knuckle down to tackle taxes, bills, and other financial papers—and because of that, it needs to have systems so that things don't fall through the cracks. While it can seem like a chore to spend time on a space that's essentially for working (and at home of all places!), the payoff to keeping your home office in check is huge.

When you think of it that way, it becomes increasingly important that you treat your home office the same way you would your office at work. Supplying yourself with the right tools—from scanner to filing systems—is an important first step to making your new organizing goals a success. A trip to an office-supply store may seem a little bit like back-to-school shopping, but wait, who didn't love back-to-school shopping as a kid? Picking out the right folders and pens might make you excited to get to those taxes this year. Hey, it's worth a shot, right?

A stylish spin on a traditional corkboard? This metal grid holds important reminders and inspiration shots with shiny metallic clips. (Opposite page) Adding overhead shelving with plenty of boxes and magazine holders is the key to banishing paper pileups on your desk.

Calendar entries:

SEPTEMBER

			1	2	3	4
						5
			school starts			
6	7	8	9	10	11	12
LABOR DAY						marlowe's party
			Test ↗		SOCCER 4PM	
13	14	15	16	17	18	19
					soccer 3.30	sleepover @ Anna's
20	21	22	23	24	25	26
				Gramma's for the Day	UPSTATE	
27	28	29	30			

EVEN IN A PAPERLESS WORLD, IT'S SOMEHOW EASY TO DROWN IN A SEA OF BILLS, LETTERS, AND FORMS. (HOW? WHY? WE DON'T KNOW.) TRANSFORM YOUR WORKING SPACE INTO A FUNCTIONAL SPACE WITH A FEW TWEAKS TO YOUR DESKTOP AND DRAWERS.

Purge That Paper

Odds are your desk is buried somewhere under mountains of paper. And some of it is probably important! Get a scanner to scan your house deed, birth certificates, etc. For each document, add a title page that says where the hard copy can be located, and send the electronic files to a secure online storage area like mozy.com, which costs about $5 a month. Bills bogging you down? Switch to paperless billing if you can. If you're not ready to switch, set a time to toss outdated documents— and to commit to purging periodically. (When the filing cabinet becomes full, some of this stash has to go.) Still tight on space? Max out your wall area by adding a row of nails to hang clipboards, where current papers can stay out in the open, but in an orderly way.

File It Away Like This

First, make sure you have these four tools: a scanner, a shredder, a filing cabinet or a file drawer in your desk, and a label maker. Documents that you're currently working on can be kept out on the desk in one shallow tray—no more than three inches tall, so it doesn't invite mess. The rest? Scan, shred, or file. Label files with a unifying category, then a subcategory. For example, instead of writing car insurance and health insurance on folders, mark them "Insurance: Car" and "Insurance: Health." That way, they all go under the letter I, and they'll be easy to find later. Only files that are somewhat active belong in the filing cabinet or file drawer.

Inventory Your Next Great Idea

As to the brilliant breakthrough you had in the shower this morning . . . and that you now can't remember for the life of you. Remember your ideas with evernote.com, a free app that you can use on any device—from a laptop to your phone. You can even take a photo of a napkin where you scribbled down the plans for your next great start-up.

Put Photos in a New Place

To get past the stalling and into a productive process, start by dumping all your photos into one container and sending them to a digitizing service like FotoBridge or scanmyphotos.com. You can create a digital library of the scanned images, then deal with the paper photos later. The next step involves man-hours, but it's worth it. Save the digital images to your desktop. Then, one by one, tag each photo with all the terms that apply: names of people, location, event type. The key is to reserve 10 minutes a day for tagging, enough to get through about 50 photos. It's a pretty mindless activity, so tag at night while watching television. Anytime you take new pictures, upload and tag them the same way. If you back them up with a service like iCloud, technically you don't have to keep the original loose pictures, which take up a lot of physical space. But it's hard to throw them out, so if you want to hold on to yours, it's easiest to sort by year and, within each year, by event.

Give Your Desk an Inbox

Seems basic, but the best way to rescue a buried desk is to funnel paper into one manageable stack that you can deal with on a regular basis. At the same time each week—say, every Sunday night before bed—take a few minutes to go through all the documents and file, toss, or shred until the inbox is blissfully empty.

File Your Email

Digital clutter is still clutter. Use a filing system like you would a file cabinet to organize the emails you need to keep. Name your files clearly so you can find the emails going forward, and for large files, break down by year or month. Think about your inbox as your online to-do list. Keep active emails in your inbox, and flag the urgent ones. Once the email is no longer timely, file into the appropriate folder, or delete out of your system.

Declutter the Cords

Wrangle loose cords with an adhesive cable holder or organizer. Or, bundle computer and other electronic cords with Velcro ties, then screw a small hook into the bottom of a desk and hang bundled wire from it, out of your sight line.

Write To-Do Lists

The act of crossing out a completed task on your to-do list gives you a major sense of accomplishment and psychologically motivates you to accomplish even more. Starting with the tasks that take only a minute or two is an easy way to get the ball rolling.

Take Care of All the Little Things

It's stressful to have to look at clutter scattered around, even when it's contained in small vessels. But if you're naturally a "dropper," the best way to cut down on the chaos is to give all the odds and ends one limited, defined amount of space. Set aside one drawer in your desk to serve as a catchall, and equip it with a multicompartment organizer. Then, whenever you're holding an item that doesn't have a clear home, put it there.

Give Yourself Receipt Relief

If your filing system is too tricky or time-consuming, you won't maintain it, so keep it simple by saving tax-related receipts in manila folders labeled by year. If you have a large volume of receipts, you might prefer an expandable folder with labeled sections, such as Business Expenses and Charitable Deductions. Use separate files for any others (for purchases you may want to return, for example). Alternatively, a digital storage system with an app like Evernote can save space. You'll need to scan any paper receipts, then slot all of them into yearly "notebooks." Keep in mind that you shouldn't be holding on to receipts indefinitely. (Three to seven years is the recommended period for tax-related ones.) To keep your collection under control, give it an annual once-over to find outdated receipts that can go.

Protect Your Passwords

If you can never remember your login to Amazon, go old-school. Rolodexes aren't just for business contacts. Use them for organizing your website log-ons and passwords.

Tech Support

THESE GENIUS APPS HELP YOU
DECLUTTER DIGITALLY.

Make a Best-of-Photo List

Start a "favorites" album on your
phone or computer, labeled by year,
and regularly move your top pictures
there as you take them. This will save
time and hassle when you need to
choose images for a class project,
a gift book for family members, or a
photo montage for a birthday.

Streamline Your Wallet

If you're bogged down with store
reward cards, it's time to go digital.
Download the iTunes app (free), take a
photo of each card and upload it, then
toss the hard copy. When you're at the
store, the bar codes can be scanned
at checkout.

Use a Pocket Scanner

Digitize papers with a mobile scanning
app such as Genius Scan (free, iTunes).
It turns your paper douments into
PDFs and JPEGs.

Organize E-bills (Almost) Instantly

Download the FileThis app (free,
filethis.com) and you can gather all
your financial docs in one spot so you
can quickly access them anywhere
(like at the bank when you're
discussing your mortgage). Select
the institutions you want the app to
collect from, enter your usernames
and passwords, and your statements
will download to a secure cloud.

Make It a Team Effort

Setting up your desk is an oddly personal thing
that's often tailored to the way your brain
thinks, so it can be tricky to share an office
space with someone else, say your artsy, right-
brained partner. Talk to him or her about your
goal for a neat, organized work area—a benefit
to both of you—and ask what steps you can
take together to make it happen. Asking rather
than dictating is more likely to get results.
Then, once you've agreed on a plan, hold each
other accountable for putting it into practice.

Shelves are Key

Hang adjustable shelves above the desk, or add
a bookcase for ample, accessible storage. Keep
things tidy with binders, magazine holders,
and boxes.

Easy Ways to Make Your Office Happier

1

Play With Light

Go with a triple threat: a floor lamp for warm-up lighting, a table lamp for a flattering glow (try a pink light bulb for even more ambience), and a small swing-arm lamp for detailed tasks.

2

Infuse the Air With Citrus

Lemon, sweet orange, and grapefruit essentials oils are uplifting. Try a diffuser, or dilute with distilled water and spray at your workstation.

3

Add Artwork

A piece of framed art gives a space a finished, homelike feel. Go for a print or a painting, which can relax and inspire while creating less visual clutter than a disarray of paper ephemera pinned to a corkboard.

4

Bring a Plant to the Table

In addition to physical benefits (all that oxygen), indoor plants may promote creativity. ZZ plants and snake plants require minimal watering and sunlight.

"Buy a clock for your office! While it seems so simple, we often don't realize how much time we waste procrastinating or spending time on social media sites. Assign a time frame for completing a task, and set an alarm to hold you accountable. You'll work through your to-do list in a more timely fashion."

—JORDAN MARKS AND CHERYL ARZEWSKI, ORGANIZERS AND COFOUNDERS OF IT'S ORGANIZED

Organize This

YOUR <u>JUNK DRAWER</u> DOESN'T HAVE TO LOOK,
WELL, JUNKY. HERE'S A SMARTER SETUP.

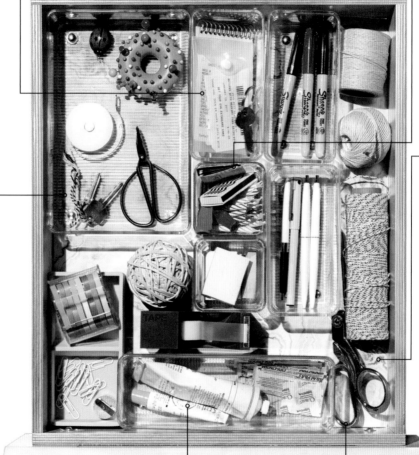

RECEIPT WRANGLER

Use a small pouch to keep all those little papers (plus coupons) from taking over. It holds about a week's worth; when it's full, it's time to toss the ones you no longer need.

MODULAR MIX

Acrylic bins let you Tetris a drawer to max out the space. Cut a piece of newspaper to fit the size of the drawer, and bring it along when you shop for drawer inserts to help you puzzle together a close fit. It's ok if they don't all fill the space exactly; gaps can hold items like rulers. Add some fun with a few creative "containers," like a doughnut eraser to hold pushpins.

BIRTHDAY KIT

Corral candles, matches, and spare balloons in one spot and—voilà—you're that pulled-together person who's always party-ready.

POP OF PATTERN

A decorative background (like adhesive wallpaper) makes this spot instantly look better. The pretty print is your keep-it-neat prompt every time you open the drawer.

GRAB-AND-GO ROW

The front section is prime real estate, so save it for the items you reach for most often: hand lotion, bandages, paper clips, lip balm. If you designate that part of the drawer as your essentials area, you'll be less likely to jam it up with random stuff.

DROP ZONE

Leave a little open space for storing odd-shaped items (scissors, rubber-band ball) and miscellaneous ones (twine for newspaper bundling, ribbon for rushed wrapping jobs).

The Tools

DESK

CABLE HOLDER

Never let your laptop charging wire fall to the floor again. A tiny cable catch keeps a cord in place while it's on your desk, but also lets you easily remove it when you're ready to go.

TRASH CAN

FILE BOXES

INBOX

Think outside the (in)box. You can use a stylish Lucite tray or even a shallow basket to store papers and folders that need to be within arm's reach.

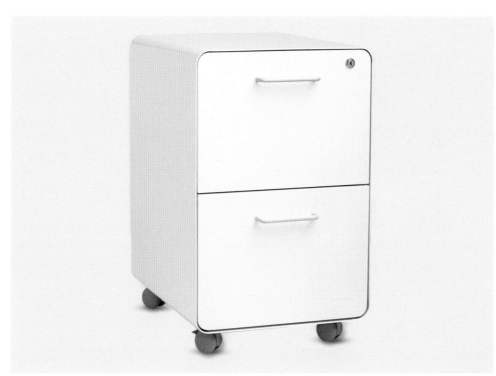

A two-drawer file cabinet comes in a million colors, can fit a ton of important docs and papers, and keeps them under lock and key. Most are even fireproof.

LABEL MAKER

STORAGE BOXES

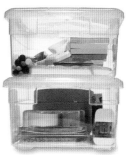

PLASTIC SHOE BOXES

SHREDDER

SCANNER

Small-Space Solutions

JUST BECAUSE YOUR HOME OFFICE DOESN'T HAVE FOUR
WALLS AND A DOOR DOESN'T MEAN IT CAN'T STILL
BE AN EFFICIENT WORKSPACE. EVEN TRUMAN CAPOTE
CALLED HIMSELF "A COMPLETELY HORIZONTAL AUTHOR"
BECAUSE HE WROTE FROM BED. HERE'S HOW TO MAKE A
SMALL SPACE WORK FOR YOU.

Shop in the Children's Aisle

If you have a little bit of room for a desk but not a
hulking piece of furniture, consider a scaled-down one
made for the younger set. Desks designed for kids and
teenagers tend to be slimmer and smaller, but most are
big enough to fit an adult chair. They also are usually
less expensive than adult desks.

Got a Wall? There's the Office

You don't need a spare room to set up an
organized workspace. An armoire or a wall
of shelving with an extra-long bottom shelf
can serve as a compact desk. This 11-inch
plank mounted on brackets is a DIY desk
(opposite page), while whiteboard paint
turns the wall into a message board.

Transform a Closet

Take the door off a space closet and you
have a great nook for getting work done.
Install a counter surface to be your desk,
and put thinner shelves above for books,
boxes, and magazine holders.

Put Paperwork on Wheels

A rolling office lets you relocate to
wherever the action is, so you can join
the family, hang out by the TV, or even sit
in the sunshine while you sort and file.
Another plus: The limited surface space
holds only essentials, preventing clutter
and prompting you to recycle as you work.

Do As Much Digitally As You Can

When physical space is at a premium,
try to keep as much of your work on the
computer as possible. A tiny desk should
ideally be able to hold a laptop, a bin for
pens and pencils, and a small notepad.

The Real Simple Method Checklist

IF YOU HAVE . . .

15 Minutes

☐ **BANISH PAPER PILEUPS.** Scan the room and notice where bills, school forms, and take-out menus have accumulated. Throw everything in a storage rack on the wall or in your inbox.

☐ **CLOSE YOUR LAPTOP.** Or, if you have a desktop, turn it off. Less visual clutter on a screen will also make the room look more serene.

1 Hour

☐ **CLEAN OUT YOUR INBOXES.** Go through the physical inbox on your desk, file the papers where they belong, and create new folders if need be. Then, take it digital and file important emails, deleting what you don't need and unsubscribing from marketing blasts.

☐ **DEGUNK YOUR COMPUTER.** Give your screen a quick wipe down with a wet wipe that's safe for electronics. Do the same with the top of your keyboard, which can collect dirt and make you feel less "together."

A Weekend

☐ **INSTALL A FILE CABINET AND MAKE A SYSTEM**. Desktop filing systems are great, but when it's time to get serious about organizing all your papers, a rolling filing cabinet is the way to go. Use hanging file folders and tabbed folders to give every piece of paper a home, and file them alphabetically. And, remember that not everything you file needs to be a filled-out form or medical record. Leave some room for blank paper, blank birthday cards, and envelopes for mailing.

☐ **CREATE AN ELECTRONICS BIN**. Gather cords, chargers, gadgets, and batteries from the random spots they occupy and give them a hidden, under-the-bed home. Line a rectangular box with a cut-to-fit rubber mat to keep items from shifting. Customize fabric drawer organizers to create large sections for bulky items like extension cords and small sections for things like cameras. Put delicately or oddly shaped items like headphones in their own nook. Clamp extension cords to keep them neat. Use rubber cord flags to mark USB wires and camera cords, labeling each with a permanent marker. Label clear pouches or small zippered bags, and fill them with memory cards, flash drives, and cartridges for video games. Separate batteries by size, and store them in the same direction. If positive and negative ends touch, it can shorten the life of the batteries.

Ask The Organizer

Q: How long should I hold onto paper items like bills or school forms before tossing them?

A: There are different guidelines for how long to keep hard copies of documents. For example:

Monthly bill statements: Switch to online versions if you can, but otherwise keep for a month, or for the current tax year if itemized for a write-off.

Taxes: The recommended time is five to seven years, and we err on the side of caution and advise our clients to maintain the documentation for seven years in the event of an audit.

Medical records: Notes on major illnesses, vaccinations, and reactions to medications should be scanned in or filed away for future reference.

—JORDAN MARKS & CHERYL ARZEWSKI,
ORGANIZERS AND COFOUNDERS OF IT'S ORGANIZED

Keep It That Way

Arranging your desk area is important, but maintaining order is just as crucial. Otherwise, when it's time to sit down to do taxes or fill out school forms, the tasks will feel even more daunting—because your first step will be clearing off space to, ya know, use the desk. Here's how to find your favorite pen every time.

Be on Drawer Duty

Every month or so, give your desk drawer a once-over and bring the hair ties upstairs to the bathroom, put the paper clips back in the desk drawer, and toss anything you realistically won't use, such as expired coupons and extra buttons. Move older files to a box in a cabinet or a closet. Annually, look at older files and shred anything that's no longer relevant. Your ultimate goal when organizing should be to find yourself with more free time. The scan-shred-file plan, if maintained, will give you just that—and a clear desk.

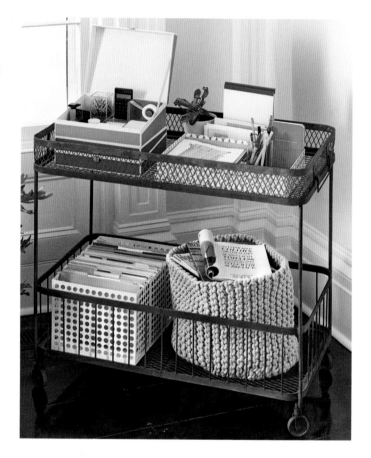

Nix the "To Be Filed" Pile

It can be tempting to put things off by making a pile of papers that need to be filed. But instead of waiting for when you have an extra ten minutes (because really, when is that going to happen?) file away papers as soon as they hit your desk and you're done using them. You'll thank yourself later.

Make a To-Do List

You're already in the right place to do it, so grab a piece of paper and write down your home office priorities, like "File away paid bills" or "Call doctor back." Not only will you feel a sense of accomplishment by crossing it off when you're done, you're teaching yourself to keep order on your newly organized desk.

THE HACK

Turn off email notifications. Those little pings are distracting and can take your mind away from the task at hand. Do it to your cell phone, too, so that you never see how many unread emails are awaiting you. That way you'll tackle them when it's time, not because you feel like you have to immediately.

Clear off the surface of your desk, even if that means neatly piling up work that you'll get back to tomorrow. Starting the day with a clean surface inspires you to get to work.

Don't Forget About Digital

So you cleaned out your email inbox—now what? Make a filing system using folders, like you would in a file cabinet, but in your email inbox. Name your files clearly so you can find emails going forward, and for large files, break them down by year or month. Only keep active or urgent emails in your actual inbox, and once an email no longer fits that description, delete it or file it in the appropriate folder.

Add a Final Step

Tell yourself that you can't step away from a project until you've shut down your computer and tidied up your desk. Leaving websites open or papers on your desk can make you feel like a project is still looming, and that'll make you less likely to want to return to it. A clean desk though? That feels like a fresh start.

Craft Room

ORGANIZING ALL THE BITS
AND BAUBLES THAT COME
WITH CRAFTING IS TRICKY.
SHOULD YOU STORE THE
LEFTOVER YARN FROM YOUR
LAST KNITTING PROJECT,
OR IS IT OK TO LET IT GO?
WILL YOU EVER REALLY NEED
THOSE GOOGLY EYES AGAIN?
HOW MANY PAINTBRUSHES
DOES ONE PERSON REALLY
NEED? INSTEAD OF EDITING
DOWN YOUR COLLECTION,
FINDING CLEVER WAYS TO
STORE WHAT YOU ALREADY
HAVE IS A SMARTER OPTION.
AFTER ALL, YOU NEVER KNOW
WHEN YOU'LL NEED TO ADD A
GOOGLY EYE TO SOMETHING.

Wrapper's Delight

Rather than let rolls rest in a random corner, set up a gift-wrap station inside a spare closet. Equip it with drawers and shelving for crafting supplies of all heights. A wall rack or a wheeled cart can corral rolls of wrapping paper. And a trunk outfitted with tension rods for ribbon easily holds clear bins with bows and cards, while casters allow it to be rolled out when needed.

Spools and Tools

If fabric and sewing supplies are spilling out of boxes and bags, you lose a lot of time having to rifle through it all to find what you need for each project. To avoid the hassle, store fabric in a drawer unit. Fold each piece into a square or a rectangle, arrange by color, and "file" like folders so you can see the fabrics' edges. If you prefer boxes for storage, keep color-coded fabric piles in stackable ones with clear, drop-down doors. Scissors, measuring tape, and other tools can stay out in the open if you store them in wall-mounted vessels or hang them on a clear pegboard. Use clear, lidded containers on open shelving for smaller items, like buttons and needles. A thread organizer will keep your spools neatly lined up. Put tiny items, like beads, in Mason jars. When screwed to the underside of a shelf, the jars won't go missing. Use larger jars for unwieldy items, like rubber stamps. Place markers and chalk in white tins that make it easy for you to see all the colors at once. Store projects, like half-knit scarves, in open baskets so you'll know where to find them.

Make Pretty, Practical Shelving

Journals, albums, and decorative items, like a shell collection, can find a home on suspended shelves. Yarn and knitting needles can occupy a little basket on one of the shelves. Or, a sleek white console tucked into dead space underneath a window can be a home for photos and scrapbooking supplies.

Keep It That Way

Make the last step of every crafting project this: Put it back, even if you're going to come back to the project the next morning. Even if it's just scissors or a ball of yarn, you'll be much more excited to start your next "crafternoon" when everything is back in its designated place.

Small Space Solutions

If an entire closet isn't an option, use a hanging shoe organizer with clear pockets to stash craft materials, and put up tension rods to hold gift wrap. Edit your collection to two rolls—one festive and one sophisticated. Or, repurpose an old dresser and dedicate a drawer for fabric, felt, and sewing supplies; use another for gift wrap. Remember, if it no longer fits, then it is time to donate or get rid of something.

The Hack

Use a wire hanger as a ribbon holder. Untwist the hanger, slide on the spools, and retwist to secure.

Ask The Organizer

Q: MY DAUGHTER'S ART SUPPLIES ARE EVERYWHERE. REGULAR BINS NEVER SEEM BIG ENOUGH, AND LARGER BASKETS BECOME A BIG JUMBLE. HELP!

A: First crack down with a clean-out. Go through all the bins and toss the junk (dried-out markers, empty glitter vials). Sort the keepers into categories—beads, stickers, paints—then give each a home. Clear containers and wall-mounted ones work best. Grouping the entire crafts stash in one art zone—say, a desk area or a bedroom corner—can keep supplies from spreading into other rooms and taking over the house.

—ERIN ROONEY DOLAND, ORGANIZER AND EDITOR IN CHIEF OF TUMBLEWEED.LIFE

Chapter 8

The Laundry Room

GET INTO THE CYCLE OF KEEPING IT ALL NEAT.

THE LAUNDRY ROOM isn't the most glamorous room in the house, and it's not like anyone (other than your family) actually sees it, so it's tempting to treat it like a junk drawer. But dropping random stuff in there like sports equipment or your gift-wrap supply "just for now" quickly clutters it up— and leaves you with a sock drawer full of singles or missing soccer jerseys on game day.

The good news? One big overhaul of your space should be all it takes to set new patterns in motion. The laundry room doesn't often get that dirty, thankfully. Take the time to spiff up the space for whomever is doing laundry, and it will make the chore less of a pain. Because as soothing as it is to press your face into a fresh stack of clean clothes and take a satisfying sniff (we all do that, right?), you've got other things to do than, well, the laundry.

Matching baskets create visual order. Assign each family member one to use as a way to transport clean clothes back to their closets. (Opposite page) Keeping surface areas clear is crucial to maintaining an efficient laundry room. Otherwise, where will you fold? It also gives you an area to pre-treat stains.

BECAUSE THE LAUNDRY ROOM IS SO UTILITARIAN, IT'S IMPORTANT TO HAVE SYSTEMS IN PLACE SO THAT YOU CAN SPEND EVEN LESS TIME IN THERE. HERE'S HOW TO NEVER LOSE A SOCK AGAIN (FOR REAL) AND GET INTO THE CYCLE OF KEEPING EVERYTHING NEAT.

Clear Everything Out

First things first: You've probably got some nonlaundry items hanging out in your laundry room. Working methodically, left to right, pull out anything not wash-related, like soccer cleats and flashlights. Then, go through the pile, discarding or donating what you don't need and storing the rest in more purposeful spots. To minimize mess, bring in three essentials: a jar to collect coins that fall out of pockets, a trash bin for lint and used dryer sheets, and a hanging mesh bag for stray socks.

Shelve What You Need

Neaten your supplies by designating a few high-up shelves or closed cabinets (out of reach from tiny ones) for detergent, bleach, and other solutions (no more than two of each; move extras to the garage). You can cut down on clothing pileups by setting your phone's timer to spur you to empty the dryer or put away clean items.

Speed Up the Process

Use baskets, rolling carts or lightweight handled hampers, one for each member of the family. Speaking of the family, do separate loads for each person, or better yet, teach the kiddos how to do their own. Keep things separate, even if you're the one doing the wash, so that you don't get bogged down with sorting. At the very least, a hamper should go in each family member's bedroom, and when it's full, they bring their dirty clothes to the laundry room and sort into whites, darks, and colors. Laundry that doesn't make it to the sorter doesn't get washed.

Set Dry Cleaning Apart

Keep dry cleaning away from the laundry room to avoid confusion. A bag with handles, kept in the closet, works well.

Designate an Ironing Station

Set a small area aside as your designated ironing area, and put an iron caddy there so that all of your goods are in one spot. The folded ironing board goes on a wall, and add a basket above to contain your iron and a bottle of distilled water or lint roller.

Line Up Your Little Helpers

Keep the essentials near the washer on a shelf preferably at eye level. (If you don't have room, try a rolling caddie that slides between the washer and dryer.) Arrange laundry products from left to right in the order you use them. For example, start with stain removers, then bleaches and detergents, then fabric softener, and lastly, spray-on starch and distilled water for ironing. Be sure to keep bleach and ammonia (found in glass cleaners) away from each other. When mixed, they can produce toxic fumes. Corral wardrobe-related items (sewing supplies, shoe polish, spot remover) on another shelf or in a clean plastic bin. If there is room, a rag, paper towels, and household-hint books can find a home here, too.

Keep a Lost-and-Found Box

Lone socks should never leave the laundry room. If a solo sock ends up in the wrong bedroom, it is less likely to be reunited with its mate. Have a collection for such socks in the laundry room, or pin them to a bulletin board.

Mount a Mini Drying Rack

If you have a standard-size drying rack that practically blocks the laundry-room doorway, swap it out for a hanging one, or buy a telescoping closet valet rod that you can install on the underside of an overhead cabinet. It's there when you need it, and it tucks out of the way when you don't.

Toss Lint

Clean the lint filter regularly. Lint buildup can clog your dryer over time and become a fire hazard. If clothes take longer than an hour to dry, lint is likely clogging the venting system. Once a year, detach the vent hose and clean it out.

The Tools

STEAMER

A steamer is like having a mini dry cleaners in your home. Just a few swipes along most garments smoothes out wrinkles, disinfects, and removes odors—all without a trip outside the house.

SHELVING

HAMPER

IRON AND IRONING BOARD

ORGANIZING ESSENTIAL

An accordion drying rack is a great way to hang your delicates or things that won't fit in the dryer. When you're done, it folds back up and can be stored out of sight.

LINT ROLLER

MESH BAG

Toss any delicate items like bras or lace undies in mesh bags to avoid them catching on other items in the washing machine.

LOOSE CHANGE JAR

Small-Space Solutions

EVEN IF YOUR LAUNDRY ROOM IS MORE OF A LAUNDRY CLOSET, THERE ARE STILL WAYS TO KEEP THE AREA FROM LOOKING LIKE IT WENT THROUGH THE SPIN CYCLE.

Section It Off

If there's no door separating your washer and dryer from the rest of your apartment, hang a tension rod and curtains to cover it up. You won't be making a sound barrier, but it'll hide the appliances and visually declutter your space.

Steam Your Clothes Somewhere Else

Keep a handheld steamer in your bathroom instead of your tiny laundry area. It's more useful when it's close to your closet because that's where you'll be pulling the items that need steaming anyway.

Look Up

Use vertical space as much as your room allows. Most washing machines and dryers sit on the floor (though pedestals are available on some models), so that means you should have room for shelving above your appliances. Store soap and other laundry-day necessities there.

Set Up a Folding Station

Washer and dryers that are front-loading and placed side by side create an instant shelf with their top surface, or a great place to install a countertop for folding. But if your model is top loading, set up a table against a wall, or better yet, install one that folds down from the wall. In a pinch, use your ironing board to fold clothes, so you can tuck it away once you are finished.

"If you need to hang clothes to dry, use a retractable stainless steel clothing line. It's more convenient and looks prettier than a permanent rod. Backs of laundry closet doors are also helpful for hanging an ironing board or additional clothes."

—JASON URRUTIA, INTERIOR DESIGNER AT URRUTIA DESIGN

The Real Simple Method Checklist

IF YOU HAVE . . .

15 Minutes

☐ **DO ONE LOAD.** Throwing one color grouping in the washer and hitting "Start" will mean fewer dirty clothes cluttering up your laundry room.

☐ **SHELVE THE REST.** Put detergent and other laundry items on the top shelf and out of the way. They don't have to be in any order—we're just doing basic decluttering here.

1 Hour

☐ **ARRANGE YOUR PRODUCTS.** Now's the time to evaluate your inventory and make a list of what you need. Line up all your products in the order you'll use them while doing the wash.

☐ **ROUND UP THE SOLOS.** Go through your bag of unpartnered socks and find the pairs. Return them to their happy homes. Keep a bag in your drawer for singletons, so if a missing sock resurfaces, you know where to find its mate.

A Weekend

☐ **MAKE SOME CHANGES.** As you go through a typical laundry routine, note where you can make changes to be more efficient. Do you need a shelf installed above the washer? A rod for hanging items that can't go in the dryer? A new hamper system? Now is the time to make those small changes that can make a big difference the next time someone goes to do a load.

The Ultimate Stain-Removal Chart

POST THIS LIST ON A BULLETIN BOARD IN THE LAUNDRY ROOM SO YOU CAN
WIPE OUT ANY SPOT, SMUDGE, OR SPLATTER THAT COMES YOUR WAY.

DRINKS

COFFEE

Boil some water and stretch the fabric over a bowl. Carefully pour the water through the stain from about a foot above. If the coffee had milk in it, follow with an oil solvent. If it contained sugar, follow with a pretreatment product and let sit for 30 minutes before washing.

JUICE

Apply a dish-soap solution (1 tablespoon clear soap in 10 ounces water). Blot to remove the stain and soap residue. If the stain remains, use a warm white towel to blot with an ammonia solution (1 part ammonia to 2 parts water).

WINE

For red wine, coat the stain with salt. Boil water and stretch the fabric over a bowl. Carefully pour the water onto the spot from about a foot above. For white wine, run cold water over the stain, then spray with a dish-soap solution (see Juice) and dab with an enzyme detergent. (Most everyday detergents contain enzymes.)

FOOD

BERRIES

Use a spatula or plastic knife to scrape off any excess. Apply a hydrogen peroxide formula (½ teaspoon dish soap and ½ cup hydrogen peroxide). Rinse.

CHOCOLATE

Scrape off any excess. Then, spray with a dish-soap solution (see Juice) and dab with detergent.

GUM

Rub an ice cube over the spot to freeze the gum, then chip away as much as possible using a spatula or a plastic knife. To loosen the remaining residue, apply a lubricant, like glycerin, then scrape it off. Rinse. If any gum remains, dab with dish soap.

ICE CREAM

Rinse thoroughly with cool water, then apply a stain pretreatment, like Shout. Fill a sink with more cool water and a few drops of detergent, and let soak.

SAUCES AND CONDIMENTS

TOMATO SAUCE

Scrape off any excess, then apply a dish-soap solution (see Juice). Blot with a damp towel to remove any residue. If the stain persists, apply a few drops of white vinegar.

MUSTARD

Flush the stain with white vinegar, then apply a dish-soap solution (see Juice), and let sit for 15 minutes.

KETCHUP

Treat with Shout. If any of the stain remains, use an eyedropper or a clean toothbrush to apply white vinegar to lighten it.

SALAD DRESSING

Sprinkle cornstarch on the spot and let sit to soak up the oil. Rinse with cool water. Apply Shout and let sit for another 15 minutes.

SOY SAUCE

Rinse stain with cold running water. Blot with ammonia solution (see Juice), then rinse again. Pretreat with Shout.

OUTDOORS

GRASS

Treat with Shout and let sit for 15 minutes. Rub in solution using a clean toothbrush.

DIRT OR MUD

Scrape off any excess once the stain is dry. Dilute a gentle detergent, like Woolite, with water and rub it on to form suds. Rinse. If any stain remains, apply a solution of 1 part white vinegar and 1 part water to lighten it.

AFTER TREATING, WASH FABRICS AS
RECOMMENDED. THE SOONER, THE BETTER!

MAKEUP

NAIL POLISH

Place the stain facedown on a clean paper towel. Apply nail-polish remover to the back of the stain. Replace the paper towels frequently to soak up the liquid. Repeat as needed. Rinse in cold water. (Note: If the fabric is acetate or triacetate, take the piece to a dry cleaner.)

FOUNDATION

Apply rubbing alcohol to the stain using a cotton swab, then blot with a cotton ball. Repeat as needed.

LIPSTICK

Spritz the spot with hair spray and let sit for 10 minutes. Wipe with a damp cloth to remove any residue and remaining stain.

HOUSEHOLD MATERIALS

CANDLE WAX

Rub an ice cube over the spot to freeze the wax, then chip away as much as possible using a plastic knife. Boil some water and stretch the fabric over a bowl. Carefully pour the water onto the spot from about a foot above.

INK

For ballpoint, create a petroleum jelly "dam" around the stain to stop it from spreading. Next, apply rubbing alcohol with a clean toothbrush. Open a window for ventilation, and dab stain with a cotton ball and mineral spirits. Let dry. Rinse with a dish-soap solution (see Juice). For permanent marker, use a clean toothbrush to rub Amodex Ink and Stain Remover into the spot.

PAINT

Use a paper towel to wipe away any dried acrylic paint or water-based paint residue. Sponge on a solution of detergent diluted with warm water. After the paint softens, remove the excess with a spatula or plastic knife. Rinse and repeat as needed.

GROSS STUFF

POOP

Scrape off any excess using a plastic knife. Turn the fabric over and rinse thoroughly with cold water. Pretreat by soaking in warm water with detergent for 30 minutes. (To disinfect completely, add chlorine bleach or color-safe bleach to the wash and launder in warm water.)

BLOOD

For a wet stain, soak in water, then dab on ammonia with a cotton swab. For a dry stain, soak in salt water for a few hours. Rinse. Treat with ammonia solution (see Juice).

VOMIT

Scrape off any excess using a plastic knife. Treat with Shout and let sit for 30 minutes. (To disinfect completely, add chlorine bleach or color-safe bleach to the wash and launder in warm water.)

BABY FORMULA

Dab with detergent. Soak for a few hours.

COLLAR RING

Pretreat with Shout. If the discoloring remains, apply ammonia if the stain is fresh, or white vinegar if the stain is old. Rinse.

PET URINE

Dab with detergent and let sit for 15 minutes.

"If you don't have time to run a full load, steam items to freshen them, release wrinkles, and kill most germs and bacteria. Follow with a spritz of fabric refresher spray, like our Fabric Fresh spray. It adds a subtle scent while removing odors."

—GWEN WHITING AND LINDSEY BOYD, CREATORS OF THE LAUNDRESS

Organize This

IS THERE ANYTHING MORE SATISFYING THAN A <u>LINEN CLOSET</u>
WITH NEAT STACKS OF TOWELS AND SHEETS?

BUY BEDDING BINS

Assign a labeled basket to each bedroom in the house, and add a set of sheets or two. You'll never have to dig through piles of mismatched pillowcases again. Or, repurpose colorful ribbons from gifts by tying them around sheet sets so individual pieces don't go stray. That way, you won't waste time hunting for matching pillowcases.

MAKE A TOWEL STASH

Stacks of washcloths and hand towels tend to topple. Instead, corral rolled ones in a wire bin. (Bonus: You can cram more in.)

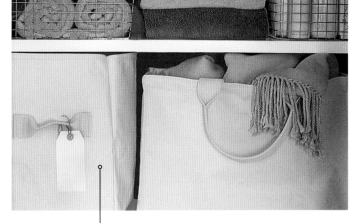

ROLL YOUR DUVET

That bulky spare comforter doesn't need to take up prime real estate. Give it a space-saving upper-corner spot after folding it in half lengthwise, then rolling it up like a sleeping bag.

KEEP A TOILETRIES KIT

A little trick with a big impact: Keep a ready-to-go grouping of soap, shampoo, and other overnight essentials so you don't have to hunt around for them every time you have weekend guests.

SUPPLY YOURSELF

You need access to bulk goods (toilet paper rolls, tissue boxes), but who wants to look at that stuff? A tall tote keeps them handy yet hidden.

Keep It That Way

Sticking to a system in the laundry room is the difference between having order over your wardrobe or never having matching socks again. Here's how to make your newly organized space work for you and your family.

IF YOU DO ONE THING EVERY DAY

No one wants to spend each day in the laundry room, but if you get the chance, clear off surfaces such as countertops and folding spaces so that you'll be ready when the next great stain strikes.

Stay Put

It can be tempting to take a laundry basket to the couch to do some folding while catching up on Netflix, but keeping everything contained inside the laundry room means less chance of losing items or failing to keep up with your system. It also keeps laundry from turning into an all-day affair.

Speaking of Folding...

Procrastinators, take note: It really does eliminate creases if you fold clothes when they're still hot, right out of the dryer. Give each item a quick shake so wrinkles don't set in. Then improve your efficiency by creating loose piles according to type: for example, T-shirts, shorts, boxers. Fold your way through each pile. By handling one type of garment at a time, you'll get into a rhythm and work faster. And when you fold like items, your stacks are neater, so they're ready for dresser drawers. (Make piles by room, of course.) If you don't have time to fold a load immediately, shake out the pieces and lay them flat in the laundry basket, one on top of another, while they await further attention.

Do A Little Inventory

Every few months or so, go through your product stash to see what needs to be replaced or refilled. Stain sticks can dry up, and almost-empty detergent bottles can be transferred to a new bottle.

Keep It Clean

Doing a deep clean every month can make all the difference in how your laundry turns out. Here's your step-by-step flow.

1

Run white vinegar through the washer to sanitize the inside and clear away soap scum. Just think, the average household washer and dryer launder about 400 full-size loads a year. That's a lot of gunk on the washer walls.

2

Empty the dryer's lint trap by wiping off fuzz with a damp cloth or a used fabric-softener sheet. Or wet your hands and run your fingers over the mesh screen to scoop up the lint. Fabric softener can cause a waxy buildup on the screen, so wash it out in a sink or vacuum it.

3

Wipe the interior walls of the dryer with a cloth dampened with dishwashing liquid and warm water. Scrub any linty residue around the trap opening with a toothbrush, if necessary.

4

Wipe down the outside of each appliance—front, sides, top, and back—with a cloth dampened with a few drops of dishwashing liquid or all-purpose cleaner.

5

Wash out the sink, if you have one, with cleaner and a cloth. Shine the faucet with a microfiber cloth.

6

Clean the countertop surfaces, shelving, and bins with a cloth and cleaner. Wipe down the cabinet fronts with a cloth and cleaner.

7

Vacuum any rugs. Mop the floor, starting from the farthest corner of the room and working toward the door. Run a dust mop underneath the washer and the dryer. Airborne lint can get kicked underneath the appliances and create a fire hazard if it piles up.

THE HACK

Decant your laundry soap into a drink dispenser with a spigot or dry detergent into a canister. It eliminates ugly bottles on your shelf.

Chapter 9

The Kids' Bedroom

CALM THE BEDROOM CHAOS, MAYBE EVEN BEFORE BEDTIME.

IT'S NO SECRET that wherever kids go, clutter usually follows. And, while it's usually the fun kind of chaos—puzzles, Legos, and stuffed animals—that creates these messes, post-play meltdowns aren't fun for anyone. Showing little ones how to be organized at an early age through your own example teaches them the importance of order, which means less time arguing when it's time to clean up—and who doesn't love that?

Rather than giving up, shutting the door, and letting the children's space become an uncontrollable clutter zone (and it's definitely tempting), putting systems into place that are easy for kids to follow is important for everyone's sanity. Color-coding can help restore order to even the unruliest toy collections, and imposing one-in, one-out rules can help keep closets from exploding. Simple rules like this are no-brainers to remember, and that means they might even carry over into adulthood, fingers crossed. Hey, they're even pretty easy for big kids to incorporate into their lives, too.

Just like in preschool, cubbies are a great system for managing tons of toys and books. For smaller metal toys, like mini cars, a magnetic strip keeps them all in one place. (Opposite page) Add wire baskets (transparent enough to see what's inside) to bookshelves so that kids can see where blocks go when they're done playing.

IF ONLY CHILDREN WERE BORN KNOWING EXACTLY HOW TO PUT AWAY THEIR TOYS AND FOLD THEIR OWN ADORABLE LITTLE CLOTHES. BUT THE GOOD THING IS THAT THEY LEARN.

Say No to Spillover

Have too many stuffed animals to fit in the toy chest? Exile some instead of starting another bin for the extras. Or, move them up to the wall. An accordion basket that expands and collapses can be nailed to the wall and accommodates growing soft-toy collections. Another great idea? Sew a piece of woolly Velcro to the back or side of each toy, then apply strips of adhesive Velcro to the wall within toddler's reach. Hello warm-and-fuzzy wall display.

Make Furniture Work Harder

Think of every surface area as an opportunity for new storage ideas. It's easy to eke out extra storage by mounting a shelf on the side of a dresser. Use it to display bedtime books in a kid's room. Do you have a red wagon that's permanently parked? Use it indoors as a stylish bookmobile. Store board books with the spines up so kids can easily see their stories.

Show Them What's Up

Kids are more likely to stay organized—and actually play with the toys—when they can see what's inside containers. But, if you'd rather camouflage the chaos, stock shelves with opaque containers labeled with graphic photos of what's inside. When it's time to swap out the Thomas trains for the Transformers, just update your shots.

Lasso in Legos

When Legos become a second carpet, buy a giant, clear, wheeled bin so it can be rolled from room to room, and dump in the general Lego bricks, keeping aside the themed kits (for example, castle or police station). Then, take each kit out of the box it came in and store it in a clear shoebox with a snap-on lid.

Organize Barbie's Accessories

Barbie's Dreamhouse can quickly become your current nightmare. To control the clutter, keep one container for dolls, one for clothing, and one for accessories. No need to overcategorize here—keeping it fun and simple for kids is best.

Corral Clothing

Have only one week's worth of outfits in regular rotation, because it's unlikely that those pants and shirts will wear out before the time comes to size up. And, instead of using hangers, which can be hard to reach and grapple with, put clothes on open shelves or in color-coded bins. It will be easier for kids to dress themselves and—fingers crossed—put their laundry away.

Share the Love

When two little ones are sharing a room, it's fine to combine their toys, but keep clothing separate. Assign specific drawers and/or shelves to each child, and if your older one is starting to dress themselves, make sure their clothes are easily accessible. Then, set up a system for transitioning clothes that are too small out of the room. Every inch of space is important, so clothing that no longer fits should be removed sooner than later. Leave a bin labeled "Too Small" in the room so that if you are in the middle of the morning routine, items can find their way to the bin immediately. Once it's full, it's time to sort and store the items.

"Teach kids that before they move from activity to activity, they need to clean up the last thing they were playing with. Nothing is worse than having every toy out of place at the end of the day. If your child is having trouble following a one-in, one-out rule, consider moving some of those newly matching bins out of reach until they can show that they know how to play with something and put it away."

—ASHLEY MURPHY AND MOLLY GRAVES,
COFOUNDERS OF THE NEAT METHOD

Organize This

SCHOOL YOURSELF ON A SMARTER
<u>KID'S DESK</u> SETUP.

ELEVATE SUPPLIES

Help keep the desktop clear by stashing grab-and-go items, like scissors and spare tape, on a pegboard or open shelves.

ELIMINATE EXTRAS

Whether they're pens and pencils or notebooks and erasers, edit supplies that have seen better days. Having fewer items in the rotation will reduce clutter and stop it from spreading to the rest of your house.

PURGE THE PAPER

Reduce the amount of paper that piles up by employing an app like Artkive (artkiveapp.com), which stores digital versions of your child's artwork.

SIZE UP

Choose a piece of furniture that will continue to work as your student grows. Seek out an option with ample drawer storage to avoid surface clutter.

ESTABLISH ORDER

Set up simple systems for your kids to follow: a tray for paper, a spot for books, a folder for finished projects. If everything is easy to find and put away, children are less likely to create a mess.

The Tools

WALL SHELF

DESK

INSTANT PRINT

Give little ones a visual clue as to what goes where. Snap a photo and print a stick-on label for bins.

DOUBLE-HANGING
CLOSET RODS

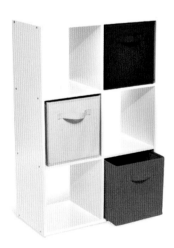

BOOKSHELF WITH BINS

WIRE BINS

HAMPER

Place a hamper in their closet where they can toss clothes they've outgrown. When it fills up, make a trip to the donation center.

SMALL HANGERS

STORAGE BIN

Small-Space Solutions

MOST TINY FAMILY MEMBERS GET THE TINIER ROOMS IN THE HOUSE, YET THEY IRONICALLY HAVE A LOT OF THINGS. BETWEEN BOOKS, CLOTHES, AND TOYS, HERE'S HOW TO MAXIMIZE A KID-PRECIOUS SPACE.

Skirt It

Most beds and cribs have room for a skirt that touches the floor—and conveniently adds extra storage for diaper stashes and toys.

Think Taller

When kids are old enough to share a room, adding a bunk bed is a great way to save on space and let the kids have a little fun come bedtime. Plus, many bunk beds have built-in, under-the-bed shelves for out-of-sight storage.

Put Up Pegboard

One large piece of pegboard is slim and can hold a ton of kids' toys (or small bins for toys). Plus, the height of the items can grow as your kids do, meaning you won't have to buy a new organizational system with each new school year.

Save an Old Coffee Table

Before you toss an old coffee table, move it to the kid's room and tranform it into a play table. The top can be a surface for trucks and doll houses, and clear bins filled with toys can go underneath.

The Real Simple Method Checklist

IF YOU HAVE . . .

15 Minutes

☐ **PICK UP PLUSH TOYS.** Quick, everyone throw stuffed animals into their bins, or arrange them on the beds, whichever's faster.

☐ **TAKE AWAY THE LAUNDRY.** Throw dirty clothes (or what's on the floor from multiple outfit changes that day) into the hamper.

1 Hour

☐ **STACK BOOKS.** Neatly file books back on bookshelves, keeping the ones that are bedtime favorites closest to the bed.

☐ **TINKER WITH TOYS.** Ensure that all toys make it to their appropriate color-coded bins. Relabel if you need to.

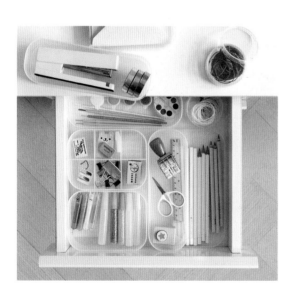

A Weekend

☐ **CLEANSE THE CLOSET.** With your little one next to you (it's important that kids see the process), take inventory of what fits, what's too small, what's had a good life (and needs to be tossed). Then, put things back, arranging by type of clothing (pants go together, same as shirts and long-sleeve Ts).

☐ **EDIT ARTWORK.** Ask your child to decide what artwork can go and what they would like stored, giving them limits along the way, like "We can keep only three drawings, so pick your three favorites."

☐ **TACKLE THE TOYS.** If something had too much love and hasn't seen a lot of playtime recently, decide (again, with your child) to toss it or donate it. Teaching kids how to part with toys, or better, give them to other kids who don't have as many toys, is a good lesson to impart early on.

Ideas for Displaying Artwork

NOT EVERYTHING YOUR CHILD BRINGS HOME CAN BE MUSEUM-WORTHY. (SORRY, BUT WE THINK YOU'LL AGREE.) HERE'S HOW TO EDIT YOUR COLLECTION AND SHOW OFF WHAT YOU LOVE.

1

Display masterpieces as they do in art galleries, with curtain wire and clips. This way, new additions can easily be swapped out with older pieces.

2

To show off art without making nail holes, create a gallery with colorful wall-safe painter's tape. You can peel off the "frames" and change the exhibit whenever your artist brings home a new portfolio.

3

For paintings you love but simply can't store or hang, scan and import them onto your computer to make a book. Now your art will be in one slim keepsake.

Ask The Organizer

Q: MY BOYS' ROOMS LOOK LIKE FIELDS OF PLANE-CRASH DEBRIS. FINDING ANYTHING IS IMPOSSIBLE, SO GETTING READY FOR SOCCER GAMES OR GUITAR PRACTICE IS INCREDIBLY STRESSFUL. THEY'RE TEENS, SO THEY WON'T TAKE ADVICE FROM ME, BUT THIS MESS IS AFFECTING ALL OF US.

A: The best approach is to pick a moment that isn't rushed and stressful, sit the boys down, and say, "Hey, it seems like it's been challenging to get out of the house. Can everybody agree on that?" Once you have a consensus, the focus shifts from any conflicts about the state of the rooms to the shared effort of problem solving. If you can get the kids to say, "Yeah, sometimes we're late because we can't find stuff," you've identified a common problem and you're on the same team. Ask them, "Any ideas?" One might say, "Well, I can never find my cleats," and you might suggest a bin by the door for cleats and shin guards. Make this as easy as possible for the kids. Even if you would prefer to hide gear in covered bins, be realistic and choose open containers, because it's a pain to remove a lid every time you need something. Of course, there's a chance that the boys won't admit to a problem. In that case, you have to play hardball. Instead of racing around with them as they get ready, and feeling like your head is going to explode, just wait in the car. Leave them to their own devices and let them be late. If and when they complain about it, you can offer to help them organize their rooms so they can get out the door more easily.

Keep It That Way

Clean Out the Closets

Make a habit of sorting through clothes three times a year: early spring, back to school, and after the holidays. If there's a sentimental dress or onesie you can't bear to send to Goodwill, pin it into a shadow box as fashionable art.

Take the Plush Toy Plunge

Yep, you can throw some toys in the washing machine. If the labels say "washable," place a few stuffed toys inside a pillowcase secured with a twist tie, then wash in cool water and Woolite. Tumble-dry on cool.

IF YOU DO ONE THING EVERY DAY

Put toys back in their bins. Middle of the night check-ins can become downright dangerous when Legos are dotting the floor.

THE HACK

Use a one-size-fits-all drawstring toy bag for speedier cleanups, and it doubles as a surface for creative kids to play.

Get the Kids to Clean Up Themselves

No really. Here's how to finally get your kids to join in on the action, no matter their age.

TODDLERS

TEACH THEM TO...Hang up coats, pull up bedding, put clothes in hamper, bring plates to sink. Toddlers think of work as play, making this the ideal time to turn what they'll think of as drudgery later into habits now. Also, following routine can give them a sense of calm, so use that to your advantage by giving your little one constant tasks that you guide them through each day.

ELEMENTARY-SCHOOL KIDS

TEACH THEM TO...Put away coat and backpack, pick up toys, clear table and load dishwasher, wipe out bathroom sink and tub, vacuum, dust, clean toilet. At this age, most kids like learning and becoming skilled at something, which makes it a great time to add some more complex jobs, like vacuuming, that go beyond picking up their own things. Even if you have a housekeeper, kids can still learn to scrub a toilet before company comes and wipe out the tub after a bath. One caveat: If you haven't been asking much of your kids before and you suddenly jump into a massive cleaning routine, it could backfire. Introduce things slowly.

TWEENS

TEACH THEM TO...Do all of the above, plus any other routine household task they haven't yet learned, like mopping the floor or doing laundry. By 11 or 12, kids are aware of how others may see them, and therefore they're more interested in their appearance, and perhaps also their home. Of course, their standards will be different from yours, but this can be an opening for chores—doing laundry or organizing the closet—that play to a desire to present their best selves.

TEENAGERS

TEACH THEM TO...Do all of the above, plus bigger jobs, like cleaning the garage, and tasks they'll need to know how to do in college. (Disinfecting a mini fridge?) By now, your teens may be more or less in the habit of putting away homework, clearing dinner, and even vacuuming on weekends. So go ahead and toss in an extra job now and then. Just don't blow your top when you find them texting, not sweeping. Teens can get distracted easily because their frontal lobes (the part of the brain governing empathy, judgment, and cause and effect) aren't fully developed yet. They still need clear directions—and patience.

Chapter 10

The Outdoor Spaces

IT'S TIME TO GET OUTSIDE FOR SOME FUN IN THE SUN.

FOR ALL OF its glorious wonders, the great outdoors doesn't offer much in the way of storage. And, if you even think about shoehorning another thing into the garage, you won't have room for the car. When it comes to organizing all the things that make the outdoors fun, you want your stuff (sports equipment, garden tools, etc.) to be accessible when you need it and easy to store when you don't. After all, tending to your garden or playing a round of badminton with the family should relieve stress, not add to it.

Thankfully, everyone can chip in to make sure soccer balls make it back into their designated bags and tools are kept in their proper spot for the next time a bike needs repairing. Plus, it's much easier to turn cleanup into a fun game (1 point for every baseball that makes it back into the bag!) when you're working with outdoor toys. And, in this kind of competition, the result is a put-together space that the whole family can use. In other words, everyone wins.

Making yourself a designated gardening center will give you perennial joy—and not just when spring hits. Keep all your essentials sorted by item, and hang tools together, too. (Opposite page) A tidy garage is a thing of joy, especially before a big home-improvement project. Clearly labeled see-through bins keep everything (including your sanity) together.

WHEN IT'S NICE OUTSIDE, THE LAST THING YOU WANT TO DO IS TIDY UP BEFORE YOUR FUN IN THE SUN. GET TO THE GOOD TIMES FASTER WITH A SYSTEM THAT'LL KEEP EVERYTHING IN ITS PLACE AND REQUIRE LITTLE TO NO UPKEEP ON YOUR DAYS OFF, WHICH YOU SHOULD BE SPENDING IN THE SUNSHINE.

Hide the Hose

Never let them see—or trip over—your garden hose. Keep it handy by hiding it in a ceramic hose pot, which looks like a pretty vase in your yard. Or, if you're just looking for a simple way to store your hose kink-free, a wall-mounted hose reel or hanger does the trick, too.

Gardening

HOW DOES YOUR
GARDEN GROW? IN AN
ORGANIZED FASHION,
THANK YOU VERY MUCH.

Gather Your Tools

When you make the
most of wall space—like
putting gardening gear on a
pegboard—your stuff stays
within easy reach, and the
space looks a lot neater. Most
hardware stores will cut
pegboard to any dimensions
you like, and a fresh coat of
paint can give it a fun pop
of color. For a smaller way
to hang, a wire cooling rack
(like what you'd rest cookies
on when you remove them
from the oven) can also
hold odd-shaped items with
hooks. And, it's not just a gem
for gardening. Keeping items
you're always looking for,
like a hammer, flashlight, or
tape measure, on a pegboard
puts them in the spotlight.

Move Work Gloves
to a Wine Rack
(Yes, a Wine Rack)

Hang the rack on the
pegboard. It's just the
right size to hold gloves,
flashlights, and other odds
and ends currently strewn
all over your workbench.

Be on the Move

A rolling tool organizer, whether you use it for gardening tools
or car doodads, has plenty of slots for tall tools, as well as
pockets for gloves and snippers. It moves from the garage to
the yard, eliminating back-and-forth trips for forgotten gear.

Pot Your Potting Soil

Bags of potting soil and fertilizer can tip over easily (and they're not much to look at anyway). Instead, pour the soil into rarely used kitchen pots with lids or cheap enamel vessels. Or, for bigger bags, go with an Oscar-the-Grouch-style garbage can.

Put a Lid on Birdseed

A galvanized metal bucket with a locking lid keeps squirrels or other critters from getting into birdseed.

Rethink Your Toolbox

Sure, a traditional tin toolbox can carry, well, tools, but it's also a great place to store small outdoor necessities like citronella candles, bug spray, and dog leashes.

Deck & Pool

MAKE A SPLASH WITH
THESE IDEAS.

Entertain With Unbreakables

No glass allowed outside; melamine dinnerware is a much better option for outdoor dining. It comes in fun patterns, is unbreakable, and can go in the dishwasher. Store it in the house when it's outdoor-entertaining season and in a waterproof plastic bin in the fall.

Prepare Grills and Propane Tanks for Winter

Before you wheel your gas grill to the garage for its cold-weather hibernation, disconnect the propane tank, which must stay outside year-round. (Propane is impervious to heat or cold, and it's illegal to put a propane tank larger than one pound in an enclosed area because it could leak and cause an explosion. Instead, keep it at least five feet from your house so that you're adhering to fire code.) After you detach it, check it for leaks by closing the valve, then sponging the valve and nozzle (where it attaches to the grill) with soapy water. If the liquid foams or bubbles, check that the valve connection is tight. If it is, you probably have a leak, and you'll need to call your dealer for disposal instructions.

Protect Yard Furniture

When summer ends, make sure the cushions are completely dry before placing them in large plastic boxes. (Poking holes in the boxes first will help prevent mildew.) Store lighter furniture, like plastic, wood, and wicker, indoors, preferably in the attic, because basements and garages can get damp. It's ok to leave heavier furniture, like wrought iron, outside, but protect it with a tarp or furniture cover with a drawstring cord. And don't forget to remove glass tabletops and store them in a safe corner where they won't be knocked over.

The Garage

MAKE ROOM FOR FUN TIMES
(AND, YOU KNOW, THE CAR).

Look Up

Technically, the ceiling is the fifth wall to your garage, and thankfully, most have plenty of vertical space for hanging bicycles, kayaks, and other large outdoor gear. Plus, hanging bikes against the far wall of the garage will help as a visual guide for pulling the car into the garage (and not tapping the back wall with your bumper). If you don't have much vertical space, try a wall-mounted track organizer, which has hooks and shelves, to hold things like a bicycle, a ladder, and garden supplies.

Stow Sports Equipment

Keep your family's gear in netted bags that can hang from hooks in the garage, or slip them into a hall closet. Stash tennis balls and baseballs in one, and a basketball in another. For bats, racquets, and golf clubs, repurpose an umbrella stand.

Ask The Organizer

Q: MY PACK-RAT HUSBAND USES OUR GARAGE AS A CATCHALL. HOW DO I DIPLOMATICALLY NEATEN IT UP?

A: In a "stuff discordant" relationship like this, the first step is to agree on a problem you can solve together. Bring it up when you're feeling connected, like after a night out. Say, "Hey, can we talk about the garage? It's getting tough to park in there, right?" When he agrees, respond, "How about we take a crack at it next weekend?" Set aside a morning or afternoon, and with a heavy-duty garbage bag and a box for recycling in hand, hunt for "low-hanging fruit"—objects that can clearly go, like a broken CD player. Seeing progress right away is motivating.

Next, lay down an old sheet and match up all the remaining items: sports gear with sports gear, lawn-care supplies with lawn-care supplies. Sorting this way gives you a clear visual of quantities, making it simpler to pull out duplicates. Narrowing down the rest is trickier. Have him pick up each item and ask, "Do I really need this? Am I keeping it for deeply sentimental reasons or just because it was pricey or a bargain?" Collect castoffs in cardboard boxes for a thrift store. The rest of the stuff will stay neater if you sort and store by category (tools, sports equipment, mementos, etc.). To get as much as possible off the floor, line the garage's perimeter with rolling metro shelves, and add clear plastic tubs labeled with the contents.

—ANDREW MELLEN,
ORGANIZER

"I love rust-proof drawer units, such as those great Bisley drawers that come in a ton of colors. I use them for my gardening tools because they're so durable. It's important that, just like in your house, you have a space in the garage for these things so that they're not just heaped. The drawers can also be repurposed in so many ways, like for storing kids' Legos, too!"

—ELLEN MADERE, ORGANIZER

Organize This

MAKE THE <u>WORKBENCH</u> WHERE YOU BUILD
PROJECTS, WELL, WORK FOR YOU.

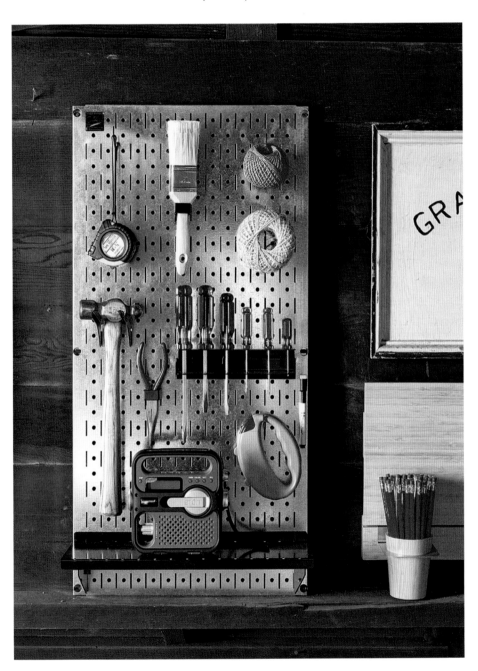

PLACE PEGBOARD

A pegboard along the wall of your workbench means everything you need will always be visible and within reach. Outline items with a paint pen while they're hanging. When they're gone, you'll have a fun visual reminder of where they go.

TIE UP TWINE

Store twine and electrical and duct tape rolls (wire spools, too) on a ribbon or rope that you can easily untie if you need to remove one. Then hang it on the pegboard.

MAKE A JUNK BOX

A tiny shelving unit is a great place to store small parts and extra nails and screws. The drawers keep it all organized.

KEEP A CLEAN SURFACE

It's hard to do any work without a clutter-free surface area. Use empty tin cans or cups to hold scissors and pencils that could otherwise muck up your work area.

Car Decluttering 101

DON'T TAKE YOUR MESS EVERYWHERE YOU GO.
HERE'S HOW TO CLEAN UP YOUR WHEELS.

Switch Gears

If you regularly leave coloring books and unfinished snack packs on the backseat for later, car clutter inevitably piles up. So put a waste can in the garage to make trash disposal automatic. Also, set a new family rule: Anything you bring into the car needs to come out when you get home. Of course, there are basic essentials that do need to be in there, like a flashlight, an umbrella, and a first-aid kit. But storing those in an over-the-seat organizer is risky—it's tempting to treat it like a catchall. Instead, opt for an out-of-the-way trunk organizer.

Move Your Castoffs to the Car

When you know there's a box or a basket in the trunk waiting for giveaways, it becomes second nature to regularly off-load old or unused items so they're not hogging space in the closets. A full container is a cue to officially let go: Bring the box to a charitable organization (like The Salvation Army), or mail it through givebackbox.com, which offers free shipping labels to send items to a local Goodwill.

Corral Loose Coupons and Store Credits

You're much more likely to cash in coupons and credits if you keep them together in one spot that's easy to access when you're shopping—and that spot is the car. Use a clear zippered envelope tucked inside the overhead visor.

Make a Plan

For overall upkeep, plan on pulling into a gas station or car wash to vacuum the car once a month. Having that on the calendar will make you more apt to keep up the decluttering in the off weeks.

The Tools

BIG PLASTIC BINS

OUTDOOR STORAGE

METRO SHELVING

STEP STOOL

If you're going to use every
square inch of your garage space,
that means building up.

A Bisley tool cabinet can hold all types of items, from tools to toys, and it keeps everything tucked away and out of sight.

BISLEY TOOL CABINET

HOSE ORGANIZER

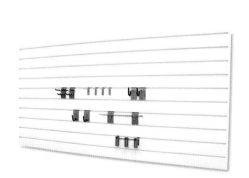

WALL BOARD AND HOOKS

CAR TRUNK ORGANIZER

MELAMINE PLATES

They're a step up from paper or plastic, are practically unbreakable, and can go in the dishwasher when the party's over.

Small-Space Solutions

Do Double Door Duty

No room for a proper tool bench and the storage that comes with it? Hang a fabric shoe organizer on the back of a door and fill it with gardening tools, spray paint cans, seedlings, and any other small items you'll want to keep handy.

Hang Chairs

Folding beach or lawn chairs don't have to lean against the garage wall, where they take up space and can fall over easily. Instead, hang them along the wall with nails.

Use Corners

Add corner shelving with plywood (or you can buy it, too) to store bottles and tools without taking up room where your car should be.

Make a Recycling-Bin Rack

On the floor, recycling bins take up too much space. Instead, prop one up on the wall between two 2x4s screwed in horizontally on the wall. Now place a 1x4 on top of the upper 2x4, and slide it down a few inches to hold the bin in place. Screw in the 1x4. Voila.

Think Outside the Garage

If you only have space for your cars inside the garage, consider an outdoor locker system that can fit your gear, withstand the elements, and has a lock for safekeeping.

The Real Simple Method Checklist

IF YOU HAVE . . .

15 Minutes

☐ **TOSS THESE FEW THINGS.** Quickly gather old newspapers, magazines, catalogs, and remnants of old DIY projects. To the trash they go.

1 Hour

☐ **ASSIGN CATEGORIES.** In the garage, give locations to these items: sports equipment, power tools, and gardening tools. Then, label the areas with blue painter's tape and permanent marker.

☐ **GIFT THE GARAGE A GARBAGE BIN.** Now you'll have a designated place to throw away food wrappers, junk you find in the yard, or other stuff from those half-finished DIY projects.

A Weekend

☐ **INSTALL SHELVING.** Metal shelving is best because it's affordable, easy to assemble, and can withstand heat and humidity better than wood. Stack waterproof plastic containers on the shelves—clear ones mean you'll always know what's inside.

☐ **DISPOSE OF OLD PAINT CANS.** Paint usually lasts for up to 10 years unopened, and 2 to 5 years if opened and stored correctly. If you don't need it on hand for touch-ups, or if it's gone bad, it's time to get rid of those bulky cans. Depending on your state, there are different laws for disposing of or recycling paint. Check to see if your state has a paint-recycling program or if there's a waste-disposal place near your home where you can drop off the cans.

☐ **RECYCLE ELECTRONICS.** Chances are you have no use for that old clunky computer, printer, and fax machine from the early '90s that have been sitting in the garage. Find a recycling program that can take them off your hands.

Q: My kids are super-helpful when it comes to gardening, but not so much for the cleanup part. How do I get them to help out for the entire time?

A: I always hear people say, "Oh my goodness, my house is like a tornado." But think about your kids' classrooms—why are they always picked up? Because before they go on to another project, they've got to put things away. We can implement that in our lives, too. Those few minutes of cleanup have to be a tag-team effort. If you're gardening with your kids and they say, "We're going to go play tennis," remind them that if they leave the tools out in the yard, they'll rust, and then no one will get to garden. They don't get a free pass, and neither should we.

—ELLEN MADERE, ORGANIZER

Keep It That Way

The garage and your gardening tools can feel a little "out of sight, out of mind," but making sure all of your tools and pool accessories make it back to their homes is really more about protecting them from the elements— and making any seasonal transition a smooth one.

Avoid Stockpiles

We say this a lot, but it's especially true when it comes to large lawn machines and bicycles. To avoid future garage pileups, commit to the "one in, one out" rule: If he brings home a new lawn mower, for example, it means you're tossing the old one.

Rotate By Season

When it's summer, make the camping equipment accessible on lower shelves, and move skis and poles to upper shelves. A switcheroo twice a year will save you time as you pack the car for a weekend campout with friends.

Protect Your Paint

To keep paint cans from going rusty, transfer leftover paint into clear, plastic, lidded containers with the paint color and finish written on top with a permanent marker.

IF YOU DO ONE THING EVERY DAY

Always make sure there's enough room in the garage to, ya know, park your car. When garages get cluttered, they lose their original purpose of housing your vehicles.

Label Everything

The best way to remember where items go (especially things like holiday decorations that only come out once a year) is to label them with a label maker or a permanent marker. You'll be happy you did so when Thanksgiving rolls around and you can't for the life of you remember where you stashed the holiday lights.

Make It a Game

There's no shame in rewarding family members who help stick to the system and put the soccer balls back in their bin. Or, make it a game by timing the kids to see how fast they can collectively clean the yard.

THE HACK

Keep loose balls of twine and rope contained. Place the balls in empty coffee cans, then use a pair of scissors to cut a slit in the plastic lid, and pull the end of the twine through the opening— instant dispenser!

Pet Areas

FIDO'S NOT MUCH OF AN ORGANIZER.
HERE'S HOW TO KEEP YOUR BEST
FRIEND'S AREA TOGETHER.

Usually, pets tend to take over lots of areas of the home, but ones who roam (cats and dogs) need a main hub for eating, like in the laundry room or kitchen. And that's usually where things go most awry, with spilling water and food. Plus, we're not dealing with a human here who can learn how to take care of him or herself. (Sadly, a game of fetch can only go so far.) It's your responsibility to devise a system that you can stick to for daily feedings and beyond.

Make a Pet Station

To deal with the graveyard of half-chewed bones and ratty sock monkeys under the kitchen table, stash your pet's goodies in a tall, skinny dresser. Dedicate the top drawer to your pet's health, with things like pills and a folder of medical records. The second drawer is for spare leashes and collars, the third for grooming supplies, and the last for bulk dog chews. Keep a dry-erase board close for important dates, like the most recent tick treatment.

Seal Up Food

As soon as you get home from the pet store, transfer any bagged dry food into a plastic container with a lid. (Plastic garbage bins work nicely.) It's not just to keep Fido from indulging—you'll also keep out other pests like mice.

Hang Your Supplies

Place a woven basket with a handle on a hook near the front door and include all you need for a dog walk: a leash, plastic bags, a few treats, and bandanas, if your dog is the stylish type. That way you'll be ready to bounce out the door as quickly as your furry friend.

Q: How do I keep a stylish home when I also have a cat who loves to claw at things?

A: Keep a cat from clawing at your new leather sofa by distracting it with other items. And not everything has to be an ugly scratch pole. Rag rugs are not-hideous ways to save your carpet (and are machine-washable) from claws. Or a cat teepee for one is a cute way to keep a feline occupied in the corner of the living room.

PETS AND PLANTS

The following are ASPCA-approved plants that are pet safe. But to train your cat out of snacking on your greenery, make the plants unappealing by spraying the leaves once a week for a period of two months with a pet-deterrent formula like Grannick's Bitter Apple Spray, and give pets something else to nibble.

Haworthia

African Violet

Boston Fern

Christmas Cactus

Parlor Palm

Hibiscus

Spider Plant

Venus Flytrap

ORGANIZING ESSENTIAL

The Modkat litter box is sleek and stylish (yes, we're talking about litter boxes here), is available in five colors, and comes with a scoop. The top-entry option means your furry friend won't be tracking litter all over your house.

How Often Should I...

REPLACE CAT LITTER

Every 3 to 4 weeks

CLEAN OUT THE FISH BOWL

Twice a week if it doesn't have a filter

WASH THE DOG

Every 2 to 4 weeks for most breeds

REPLACE HAMSTER BEDDING

Weekly

REPLACE BIRD CAGE LINER

Every day

Banish Pet Hair

You know it's bad when your coworkers can tell you have a pet because they can see the dog hair on your sweater. Before laundering your clothes, use a lint brush to remove as much of the hair as possible. Then wash using an animal-specific detergent that's rich in enzymes; these cleaners break down hair and lint better than traditional laundry soaps. While the clothes are still damp, use a lint brush again to remove any last remaining hairs.

Hide a Litter Box

Keep a cat's box in an area that's near a trash can and won't stink up the house, like a laundry room. (You can also store litter there.) Or a paneled private commode, available at most pet stores, can conceal an entire litter box—the hole in it lets your cat in and out.

Keep It That Way

Pets make messes no matter where they go. Keep your home under control from pet dander with regular vacuuming to prevent guests from asking, "Do you have a dog?" based on smell alone. Then make sure to launder pet beds every couple of weeks or so with a gentle detergent.

How to Fix Common Pet Messes

Feathered and furry family members are cute, but they can also be pigs. These cleanup strategies should help.

1
DIRTY CAGE

A daily wipe-down with a damp paper towel is the best way to clean droppings from a hamster, a rabbit, or another small animal. That way the dropping won't turn to dust that can be inhaled. Be sure to dry it thoroughly afterward, as a cage with damp spots can quickly grow mold (also true for crates and kennels). For a deeper cleaning (at least once a week), mix drops of dish soap in a bucket of warm water and scrub the entire surface with a nylon-bristle brush. Rinse with a handheld showerhead or a garden hose to reach the corners. Dry completely with a paper towel, or let sit in the sun for an hour.

2
RAUNCHY PET BED

Bathing your pooch at least once a month (if vet-approved) can keep doggie stench at bay. Wash the bed on the same day, so the dog doesn't contaminate his clean sleeping spot. (A bed with a machine-washable shell and cushion is, obviously, easiest.) First vacuum the shell to remove as much fur as possible. Then toss both pieces in the washing machine and clean with laundry detergent plus four squirts of an odor eliminator.

3
STINKY LITTER BOX

Litter upkeep is cringe-worthy but crucial: Even small traces of pet waste can carry harmful viruses, bacteria, and parasites. (Plus, the odors!) At least once a day, scoop out any clumps. Do a full cleaning as needed or at least every few weeks: Dump all the old litter into a large trash bag, then scrub the pan and the lid with hot, soapy water using a nylon-bristle brush. Rinse with a hose or under the faucet of a utility sink; dry fully with a paper towel before refilling with two inches of fresh litter.

4
GRIMY TOYS AND FOOD BOWLS

A monthly cleaning will reduce dirt and bacteria buildup on toys. Most cloth toys can be machine-washed on a cold cycle; place them inside a pillowcase first. Chew toys (such as treat stuffers) that get gunky can typically go in the dishwasher. Toss food and water bowls into your daily dish-washing cycle; or rinse with hot, soapy water and dry thoroughly.

5
FUR-COVERED FURNITURE AND RUGS

A rubber squeegee is the best tool to get floor coverings clean. Rub it over a rug; the friction will push the hairs into easily disposable piles. On upholstered furniture, swap the squeegee for a damp rubber glove—the method is the same. To cut down on pileups in the first place, it's helpful to brush cats and dogs regularly: a couple of times a week for long-haired pets and about once a week for short-haired ones.

6
STAINED CARPET

Tracked-in mud is easier to remove if you let it dry first. Once it's dry, brush off or vacuum up as much as you can, then treat the stain with laundry detergent, blotting with a damp paper towel. To eliminate a fresh urine stain, lay a stack of paper towels over the spot, then stand on top of it to soak up the liquid. Next, use a cotton cloth to apply a mixture of ¼ teaspoon dish soap and 1 cup warm water, then blot with a fresh paper towel; repeat until no color or smell remains. For older stains, apply an enzyme-based cleaner, which will break down the organic proteins.

Our Experts

JENI ARON is a professional organizer who owns and operates Clutter Cowgirl Professional Organizing in New York City.

LAYNE BROOKSHIRE is the founder of Ms. Placed Professional Organizing in Austin, Texas.

ERIN ROONEY DOLAND is a de-cluttering pro from the Washington, D.C. area. She is the author of *Never Too Busy to Cure Clutter* and *Unclutter Your Life in One Week*, Editor in Chief of Tumbleweed. Life, and Editor-at-Large of Unclutterer.com.

JORDAN MARKS AND CHERYL ARZEWSKI are the cofounders and owners of It's Organized, a home organization company in New York and California.

ELLEN MADERE of EllenGetsItDone.com is a Connecticut-based professional organizer.

ANDREW MELLEN is a New York City-based organizing and time management expert, blogger, podcaster, and author of *Unstuff Your Life!*

ASHLEY MURPHY AND MOLLY GRAVES are cofounders of NEAT Method, a lifestyle service that provides luxurious and smartly appointed living spaces around the country.

JASON URRUTIA is an interior designer and principal at Urrutia Design based in Sausalito, California.

GWEN WHITING AND LINDSEY BOYD are the cofounders of The Laundress, an eco-friendly line of home and fabric care products.

ALEXANDRA WILSON is an entrepreneur and cofounder of online shopping company Gilt, on-demand beauty service GLAMSQUAD, and closet-styling company Fitz.

LISA ZASLOW is a professional organizing consultant, the founder of Gotham Organizers in New York City, and the author of *Can't I Just Shred It All? 101 Quick Tips to File—and Find—Your Important Papers.*

Resources

WHERE TO BUY ITEMS
FEATURED IN THIS BOOK

Bedding

ABC Carpet & Home
abchome.com

Brahms Mount
brahmsmount.com

The Company Store
thecompanystore.com

Kerry Cassill
kerrycassill.com

Serena & Lily
serenaandlily.com

Roller Rabbit
rollerrabbit.com

Closet Essentials

Amazon
amazon.com

Bed Bath & Beyond
bedbathandbeyond.com

Closet Maid
closetmaid.com

The Container Store
containerstore.com

Improvements
improvementscatalog.com

LA Closet Design
shoplaclosetdesign.com

Organize-It
organizeit.com

Target
target.com

Furniture & Storage

CB2
cb2.com

Cost Plus World Market
worldmarket.com

Crate & Barrel
crateandbarrel.com

Design Within Reach
dwr.com

IKEA
ikea.com

One Kings Lane
onekingslane.com

Overstock
overstock.com

Pottery Barn
potterybarn.com

Rejuvenation
rejuvenation.com

Wayfair
wayfair.com

West Elm
westelm.com

Williams Sonoma Home
williams-sonomahome.com

Curtains & Drapes

Loom Decor
loomdecor.com

Restoration Hardware
restorationhardware.com

The Shade Store
theshadestore.com

Kids Room

The Container Store
containerstore.com

Crate & Kids
crateandbarrel.com/kids

Gautier Studio
gautierstudio.com

Ikea
ikea.com

Pottery Barn Kids
potterybarnkids.com

School Outfitters
schooloutfitters.com

Swoop Bags
swoopbags.com

Kitchen Essentials

Bed Bath & Beyond
bedbathandbeyond.com

Brook Farm General Store
brookfarmgeneralstore.com

The Container Store
containerstore.com

Crate & Barrel
crateandbarrel.com

OXO
oxo.com

Sur La Table
surlatable.com

Williams Sonoma Home
williams-sonoma.com

Lighting

Cedar & Moss
cedarandmoss.com

Circa Lighting
circalighting.com

Finnish Design Shop
finnishdesignshop.com

Schoolhouse Electric & Supply
schoolhouse.com

Shades of Light
shadesoflight.com

YLighting
ylighting.com

Office Essentials

Poppin
poppin.com

Staples
staples.com

Three by Three Seattle
threebythree.com

Pillows

John Robshaw Textiles
johnrobshaw.com

Judy Ross Textiles
judyrosstextiles.com

Lulu and Georgia
luluandgeorgia.com

Urban Outfitters
urbanoutfitters.com

Outdoor Storage

Home Depot
homedepot.com

Improvements
improvementscatalog.com

Organize-It
organizeit.com

Tabletop Accessories

Canvas Home
canvashomestore.com

Crate & Barrel
crateandbarrel.com

Fishs Eddy
fishseddy.com

Global Table
globaltable.com

Credits

Selected Shopping Credits

Amazon.com: BoxLegend T-shirt clothes folder (p. 132); Yamazaki Tosca Storage Basket (back cover)

Bed, Bath, & Beyond: Real Simple flocked suit hangers (p.28, p. 133); Salt cabinet shelf riser (p.82); Real Simple garment storage underbed bags, Real Simple organizer, Real Simple triple laundry sorter (p. 133); Camarillo marble vanity tray, InterDesign over the door towel rack and hook (p. 154); Polder® Styling Station (p. 151) Rowenta Master 360 Garment Steamer, Real Simple Ironing Board, Bonita Wonderwall Wall-mounted Drying Rack and Real Simple Wash Bags (pp. 202-203); Prostate Sports Bundle Wall Board and Home Basics Foldable Trunk Organizer (p. 251)

Bluewinkdesigns.etsy.com: Personalized kid's chore chart (p.16)

CB2: Solid brass studio storage box set (cover, p. 53); Loki blush leather pillow (front cover); beam floor lamp (p. 52); aluminum large gold tray (p. 53); canary round marble trivet and hat trick vase set (p. 105);

The Container Store: Bigso Stockholm desk files (cover); Velcro Cord Holders (p. 53); expandable bamboo utensil tray, InterDesign silver open stackable baskets, Elfa utility wire kitchen door and wall rack (p. 82); 2-Tier Stainless Steel Lazy Susan, InterDesign Deep Fridge Binz (p. 83); Anchor Hocking Montana Glass Canisters (p. 83, back cover); Hagerty 6-Piece Silver Place Setting Roll (p. 104); clear shelf divider (p. 132); InterDesign Linus Medicine Cabinet Organizer (p. 154); Yamasaki Large Adhesive Web Cable Holder (p. 178); orange & pink large striped canvas storage bin with handles and Joy Mangano kid's huggable hangers (p. 225); rainbow 9-drawer storage unit (p. 225);

Crate & Barrel: Dearborne bench (p. 29); dinnerware storage set (p. 105); teak ladder rack (p. 155); honeycomb yellow hexagon shelf and Taylor walnut desk (p. 224); Caprice Medallion melamine plates (p. 251)

Flint: Flint Lint Roller (p. 203)

IKEA: Risatorp Baskets (back cover)

Kaufmann Mercantile: MINNA pillow (front cover)

Michele Varian: Funnel Retro Industrial Pendant Light (front cover)

ModKat: Modkat litter box (p. 262)

Office Depot: DYMO MobileLabeler (p. 179)

Poppin: White stow 2-drawer file cabinet (p. 179)

Rejuvenation: Vernon bin pull and knob hardware (front cover); Ash Wood & Leather Nesting Baskets (front cover, p. 29, back cover); cablelock wool basket (p. 52)

Serena & Lily: Cushion fabric and tassel pillow (front cover)

Swoop Bags: Original Swoop Bag (p. 233)

Target: Made By Design Aluminum Shower Caddy (p. 154); Made By Design Metal Mesh Storage Bins (p. 225); Made By Design 5-Tier Metal Shelving Unit (p. 202)

Umbra.com: Estique key hook and organizer (p. 29)

West Elm: Metalwork Console (p. 28); Mid-Century Coat Rack (p. 28); Parker Slipper Chair (p. 52); Industrial Storage Coffee Table (p. 53); Mid-Century Buffet and Mid-Century Storage Bench (p. 104), Contemporary Upholstered Storage Bed (p. 132); Portside Outdoor Storage Trunk (p. 250)

Additional Photo Credits

William Abranowicz (pp. 36, 48, 60, 125, 200, 236); ACP/Trunk Archive (p. 167); Africa Studio/Shutterstock (p. 164); Lucas Allan (p. 173); Anna-Alexia Basile (pp. 9, 51, 86, 174); Adobe Stock (pp. 203, 250); Alpha Smoot (pp. 123, 131, 177); Aluxum/Getty Images (p. 84); Burcu Avsar/Offset (pp. 154, 256); Sidney Bensimon (pp. 145, 153); Biz Jones/Offset (p. 201); Levi Brown (pp. 82, 179); Hallie Burton (p. 230); Ashley Capp (p. 206); Lucia Coppola/Shutterstock (p. 22); Corbis/Getty Images (p. 172); Kim Cornelison (p. 79); Grant Cornett (pp. 29, 132, 154, 178); Francis Dzikowski/OTTO Archive (p. 66); Aaron Dyer (pp. 224, 263); illustrations by Eight Hour Day/Katie Kirk (pp. 208-209); Epoxydude/Getty Images (p. 179); Experience Interiors/Getty Images (p. 38); Mike Flippo/Shutterstock (p. 82); Floto + Warner (pp. 42, 94, 128, 129, 139, 143); Phillip Friedman (pp. 82, 154); Thayer Allyson Gowdy (pp. 55, 63, 107, 116, 181); Bryan Gardner (pp. 192, 258); Jack Gardner (pp. 194); Alice Gao (p. 158); Getty Images (pp. 179, 261); Laurey W. Glenn (pp. 126, 180, 196); Lenora Gim/Getty Images (p. 220); John Gruen (p. 248); Randi Brookman Harris (p. 223); Hero Images/Getty Images (p. 140); Raymond Hom (pp. 57, 160); The Home Edit (p. 105); Karl Juengel (p. 82); Dean Kaufman (p. 45, 97, 106); Manfred Koh (pp. 28, 179); Erin Kunkel (pp. 54, 74, 98, 122, 238); Francesco Lagnese (pp. 11, 47, 214, 229, 231); John Lawton (p. 104); Mark Lund (pp. 221); Charles Masters (p. 105); David Meredith (pp. 4 101); James Merrel (p. 182); Johnny Miller (pp. 28, 31, 35, 39, 72, 76, 86 top, 87, 120, 121, 132, 136 top, 150, 217); Leslee Mitchell/Offset (p. 108); Jens Mortensen (pp. 132, 147, 179, 251, 260); Aaron Cameron Muntz (p. 134); Tessa Neustadt (pp. 40, 70, 95, 111, 112, 137, 228, 234); Fran Parente/OTTO Archive (p. 187); José Picayo (pp. 58, 190); David Prince (pp. 75, 98, 186, 219); Studio McGee (p. 204); Tessa Neustadt (pp. 40, 70, 95, 111, 112, 137, 228, 234); TaraPatta/Shutterstock (p.28); Richard Peterson/Shutterstock (p. 28); Paul Raeside (p. 109); Travis Rathbone (p. 252); Trinette Reed/Stocksy (p. 159); Lisa Romerein (pp. 68, 71, 77, 216, 254); Matt Sartain (pp. 18, 157, 162, 213); Annie Schlecter (p. 32); Joe Schmelzer/Offset (p. 108); Eira Sophie/Getty Images (p. 243); Shutterstock (p. 261); Kevin Sweeney (pp. 225, 233); Erin Swift (p. 146); Christopher Testani (p. 20); TS Photographer/Shutterstock (p. 251); Jonny Valiant (pp. 2, 21, 23, 33, 69, 73, 144, 148, 149, 156, 168, 171, 188, 191, 199, 207, 212, 218, 227, 228 bottom, 237, 240, 241, 242, 245, 247, 250, 253, 255, 259); Andreas von Einsiedel/Getty Images (p. 90); Björn Wallander (p. 46); Valerie Wilcox/Offset (p. 24); Anna Williams (p. 6, 56); Matthew Williams (pp. 30, 85, 99. 138 189, 198, 211, 232); James Wojcik (pp. 29, 154, 193); Yippun JJ/Shutterstock (p. 28); YoungHouseLove.com (p. 64)

Index

A

apps
  Artkive (artkiveapp.com), 223
  Basil, 79
  Eat Your Books (eatyourbooks.com), 79
  Evernote (evernote.com), 79, 170, 173
  FileThis (filethis.com), 174
  Finery (finery.com), 138
  F.Lux (justgetflux.com), 122
  Paperkarma (paperkarma.com), 174
  Paprika Recipe Manager
    (paprikaapp.com), 79
  Sleep Cycle, 122
  White Noise, 122
artwork, 175, 230
  minted.com, 61
  theposters.co 61
  sorting and storing, 228
  Tappan Collective, 61
  20x200.com, 61
Arzewski, Cheryl, 176, 185
Ask the Organizer
  Aron, Jeni, 113
  Arzewski, Cheryl, 185
  Brookshire, Layne, 161
  Doland, Erin Rooney, 59, 193
  Madere, Ellen, 257
  Marks, Jordan, 185
  Mellen, Andrew, 245
  Wilson, Alexandra, 135
  Zaslow, Lisa, 89

B

Barbie, 219
bar cart, 30, 103. *See also* **rolling**
  cart; tiered cart
Bar Keepers Friend, 72
baskets
  in entryway, 19–25, 27–33, 35
  pull-out, 158
  three-tier wire, 84, 151
  under-the-sink, 154
Bathroom, 140–163

bed
  bunk bed, 227
  making every day, 118, 136, 139
  mattress, freshening, 139
  and storage, 118, 121, 132, 133
Bedroom, 114–139. *See also* **bed;**
  Kids' Bedroom
bench
  in entryway, 22, 24, 25, 34
  with hidden storage, 29, 43, 98, 104
bicycles, 30, 245
birthday kit, 177
Bisley tool cabinet, 246, 251
blankets, 40, 43, 56
  Pattern Combos That Work, 49
board games, 44, 54, 57
  Game Savers storage units, 44
bookends, 51
books, 22, 24, 54, 56, 62, 117, 223, 228
  donating, 14, 57
  as hidden storage, 46
  organizing in a bookcase, 38, 51, 57
  scanning artwork and photos to
    make a book, 174, 230
bookshelf, 224
boots, 21
  in entryway, 23, 24, 25
  storing, 27, 28, 32, 35, 126

C

camping equipment, 258
candles
  citronella, 241
  storing, 76, 98
candlesticks, 13
Car Decluttering 101, 249
cats, 261–263
chalkboard wall, 75
china
  cabinet or buffet, 97, 104, 110
  caring for, 109
  displaying, 97, 102
  storing, 97, 105
Chore Chart, 16

cleaning
  bathroom, 162
  bed linens, 139
  chandeliers, 110
  computer, 182
  entryway, 32, 34
  furniture, 62
  heating and AC vents, 65
  kid's room, 233
  lamps and lamp shades, 65
  laundry room, step-by-step, 213
  Makeup Brush Cleaning 101, 147
  moldings, 65
  remotes, 64
  routine for kitchen, 91
  rugs, 110
  scuff marks, 35
  slipcovers, 63
  sofas, 63
  speakers, 64
  stovetop, 91
  stuffed animals, 232
  switch plates and doorknobs, 35, 65
  TV, 64
  window treatments, 65
cleaning supplies
  glass cleaner, 158
  Mr. Clean Magic Eraser, 35
  storing, 78, 149
clock for office, 176
Closet, 124–131, 228. *See also* **hangers**
  A Clean-Sweep Checklist, 129
  clothing rods, 124, 128, 224
  gift-wrap station in, 189
  as home office, 180
  lights in, 139
  organizing, 130
  out-of-season clothes, 127
  overhaul, 137
  shoe organizer, 133
clothes
  donating, 14
  keepsake, 232
  storing in zippered vacuum bags, 33

Clutter Cowgirl, 102, 113
clutter, eliminating, 21, 23, 97, 118, 172
coat rack, 24, 28, 32, 35
coffee table, 40, 54, 56
  clearing off every night, 38
  in kid's room, 227
  with storage, 40, 53
color-coded
  hangers, 33
  electrical cords, 57
composting, 77
computer, 180
  cleaning, 182
  shutting down, 187
  storing photos on, 174
containers. *See also* **baskets; storage**
  acrylic bins, 177
  apothecary jars, 145
  boat totes, 17
  caddies, 151, 154, 156, 199
  clear, 68, 87, 127, 132, 145, 225, 237
  clear canisters, 153, 154, 158
  clear, lidded, 190, 219
  clear plastic bins, 83
  clear zippered envelope, 249
  color-coded bins, 220, 228
  decorative boxes, 51, 53, 96, 167, 174
  electronics bin, 183
  Mason jars, 190
  open-weave metal bins, 27
  plastic, 27, 151, 251, 254, 261
  plastic shoe boxes, 179
  red wagon, 218
  toolbox, 241
  toy chest, 218
  for umbrellas, 32
The Container Store, 33
corkboard, 167, 175
countertops, 70, 86, 91
  keeping clutter-free, 80, 90
Craft Room, 188–193
  gift-wrap station, 189
crystal and glassware, 103
cubbies
  in entryway, 20–22, 27, 33, 35
  in kid's bedroom, 217, 225
  for shoes, 126

D

Deck & Pool, 242–243
  outdoor storage, 250
desk, 178
  clearing off surface, 187
  DIY, 180
  kid's, 180, 224
  maintaining order, 186
  shelving as, 180
digital clutter, 170, 174
digital storage system, 173
Dining Room, 92–113
  4 Ways to Set Your Table, 100
dishwasher, 17, 86, 242
Dishwasher Do's and Don'ts, 88
dog leash, 23, 27, 241, 260
donating, 12, 14, 57, 146, 198
  blankets, 43
  books, 62
  Charity Concerns, 14
  extra toiletries, 146, 161
  givebackbox.com, 249
  outgrown kid's clothes, 225, 232
  pots and pans, 87
  Where to Donate (chart), 14
  Where to Sell (chart), 15
drawers
  acrylic bins for, 177
  in closet, 129
  organizers, 72, 121, 145, 172, 183
  for storing candles, place mats, containers, 76
  T-shirts, filing vertically, 121, 132
dresser
  clearing off surface, 121, 136
  floating, 117
  in kid's bedroom, 224
  mounting a shelf on the side, 218
  moving off-season items from, 121
  for storing pet supplies, 260
dry cleaning, 13, 199
dry-erase board, 23, 29, 260
  DIY, 29
DVDs, 43, 54, 170

E

electrical cords, 172, 183

adhesive cable clips, 43
cable holder, 172, 178
ID each cord with a tag, 43
organizing, 43, 57
plastic zip ties, 43, 53, 57
Velcro cord holders, 53, 172
electronics
  bin, 183
  recycling, 254
electronic storage
  iCloud, 170
  mozy.com, 169
emails
  managing, 170, 187
  online to-do list, 170
  turn off notifications, 186
Entryway, 18–35

F

family, involving, 16–17, 32, 35, 228, 231
  assigning hangers, 27, 33
  assigning hooks, 23
  assigning laundry hampers, 199
  in gardening cleanup, 257
  involving teens, 231
  "no shoes indoors," 34
  separating kids' things from big kids' stuff, 27
  weekly search-and-recovery day, 27
filing cabinet, 169, 170, 183, 187
Fitz, 130, 135
flashlights, 198, 240
flowers, in entryway, 24, 25, 32
folding board, 132
furniture
  arrangement of, 22, 40
  beanbag, 54
  chair, 54, 121
  cleaning, 62
  with hidden storage, 46
  kid's desk, 223
  multitasking, 118, 134
  outdoor, 242
  sofa, 61, 63
  stool, 54
  wicker, 62

G

Gallery Wall 101, 61
Garage, 236, 244–245, 250–255
garden hose, 239, 251
Gardening, 237, 240–241, 252
 getting kids to help with cleanup, 257
 supplies, storing, 241, 245
 tools, storing, 237, 246
Goodwill, 14, 232, 249
Gotham Organizers, 80, 89
Grannick's Bitter Apple Spray, 261

H

The Hack
 bathroom: rub dampened dryer
  sheet over wet shower door to
  banish soap-scum buildup, 163
 closet: hang three-tiered wire basket
  in, 138
 craft room: wire hanger as ribbon
  holder, 193
 dining room: keep handheld vacuum
  near china cabinet, 110
 entryway: hang wet coats in shower, 34
 home office: turn off email
  notifications, 186
 kid's room: label toy bins and shelves
  with bright-colored washi tape
  and permanent marker, 233
 kitchen: stash extra trash bags at
  bottom of garbage can, 91
 laundry room: decant laundry soap
  into drink dispenser with spigot, 213
 living room: open and close window
  treatments to displace dust, 65
 outdoor spaces: empty coffee cans as
  twine and rope dispensers, 259
hamper, 17, 127, 199, 202, 228
 built-in, 142
 for outgrown kids clothes, 225
 three-part, for sorting, 133
handbags, 127
 Organize This, 131
hangers, 124
 alternatives to, for kid's clothes, 220
 color coded, 27, 28, 33
 small, for kid's closet, 224

 for storing out-of-season clothes, 127
 velvet slimline, 133
hanging organizer, 27, 44, 193
hanging shelf, 23
hardware store, 33, 149, 240
Home Office, 164–193
 artwork in, 175
 rolling, 180
homework, 96, 110
hooks, 17, 20, 21, 29, 32, 68, 172
 adhesive, 72
 in entryway, 25, 29, 33, 35
 in garage, 245
 for hanging pots and pans, 72
 for keys, 23, 29
 over-the-door, 154
 picture ledge with, 30, 33
 S-hooks, 156
 for storing jewelry, 126
 for towels, 72, 151
**How Often Do I Really Need to
 Replace That? (chart), 146**
How Often Should I...?, pet edition, 262
**How Often Should I Wash My... bed
 linens?, 139**

I

If You Do One Thing Every Day
 clear off coffee table, 62
 clear off countertop, 90
 clear off surface areas in laundry
  room, 212
 clear off surface of your desk, 187
 clear out items that don't belong in
  dining room, 110
 make sure there's room in garage to
  park your car, 258
 make your bed, 139
 put toys back in their bins, 232
 sort mail, 35
 wipe down sink hardware, 163
inbox, 170, 178
 cleaning out, 182
 email, 187
ironing
 board, 202, 204
 station, 199
It's Organized, 176, 185

J

jewelry, 126, 134
junk box, on the workbench, 247
junk drawer, 12, 177
junk mail, 23, 32
 permanent end to (paperkarma.
  com), 33, 174

K

keys, 22, 27, 30, 131
Kids' Bedroom, 214–233
Kitchen, 66–91
 hot zone, 70
 pull-out organizer, 78
 sink, 78, 89, 91
knives, 74

L

label maker, 17, 33, 90, 179, 259
labels, 17
 for electrical cords, 183
 for files, 170, 173, 187
 for food in freezer, refrigerator, and
  pantry, 83
 for holiday decorations, 259
 for hooks, 23, 33
 for just-opened products, 146
 for paint cans, 258
 "period after opening," 144
 photos of toys on containers, 218, 224
 for refrigerator bins, 81
 for spices, 84
 for stored china and crystal, 97
The Laundress, 210
laundry
 hampers for, 127, 133
 sorting, 142, 199
 teaching kids to do their own, 199
Laundry Room, 194–213
 folding station, 204
 keeping surface areas clear, 196
 lost-and-found box, 200
 mini drying rack, 201
 rolling caddie, 200
Lazy Susan, 78, 83
Legos, 219, 246

lighting
    bedroom, 119
    cleaning, 110
    in closet, 27, 139
    floor lamp, 52
    for home office, 175
    living room, 44, 47
    table lamp, 45
    under-cabinet, 74
    wall mounted, 106, 134
linen closet, 148, 151, 211
linens, 98, 109
lint roller, 203
Living Room, 36–65
lost-and-found box, 200

M
magazines, 22, 32, 40, 56, 96
    recycling, 56
magnetic
    baskets, 30
    organizers, 145
    strip, 153
    tins, 84
mail, 22, 30, 110. *See also* **junk mail**
    sorting, 32, 35
makeup, 144, 145, 147
medical records, 185
    for pets, 260
medicine cabinet, 145, 148, 156, 158
    Organize This, 153
mirror, 28, 30, 54, 106, 148
    cleaning, 32, 158
    in entryway, 24
    full-length, 156
    hidden storage in, 156
movie night, 38, 40, 62
Ms. Placed Organizing, 152, 161
mudroom. *See* **Entryway**

N
NEAT Method, 222
Netflix, 43
newspapers, recycling, 56
nightstands, 117, 119, 132, 134

O
one-in, one-out rule, 62, 138, 222, 258
Organize This
    bar cart, 103
    bookcase, 51
    coat closet, 27
    handbag, 131
    junk drawer, 177
    kid's desk, 223
    linen closet, 211
    medicine cabinet, 153
    refrigerator, 81
    undie drawer, 123
    workbench, 247
Organizing Essential
    accordian drying rack, 203
    bench with hidden storage and
      shelf, 29
    Bisley tool cabinet, 251
    coffee table with storage, 53
    ladder towel rack, 155
    Lazy Susan, 83
    Modkat litter box, 262
    quilted china storage bag, 105
    see-through containers in kid's
      bedroom, 225
    two-drawer file cabinet, 179
    velvet slimline hangers, 133
ottoman, 43, 45, 47
Outdoor Spaces, 234–263
    making yard cleanup a game, 259
    toolbox, for outdoor supplies, 241

P
paint
    disposing of old cans, 254
    storing, 254, 258
    whiteboard, 180
pantry, 78, 83, 86, 87
paper
    holding onto bills, school
      forms, 185
    Paperkarma® app, 33
    purging, 169, 223
passwords, managing, 173, 174
pegboard, 190, 223, 227, 240, 247
Pet Areas, 260–263
    ASPCA-approved plants, 261
    Grannick's Bitter Apple Spray, 261
    How Often Should I..., 262
    Modkat litter box, 262
photos, 33, 43, 54
    creating scrapbooks, 170
    digitizing service for, 170
    Gallery Wall 101, 61
    scanmyphotos.com, 170
    socialprintstudio.com, 54
    storing electronically, 170, 174, 230
    tagging, 170
picture frames, 22, 57
    alternatives to, 54
pillows, 56, 137
    Pattern Combos That Work, 49
Post-it notes, oversize, 76
Post-it notes, Super Sticky, 12
Pro Tip
    buying a clock for your office, 176
    displaying china, 102
    freshening clothes when there's no
      time to wash them, 210
    fitting everything in space allotted or
      let it go, 26
    hang clothes to dry, 205
    hotel mini products, 152
    keeping countertops clutter-free, 80
    organizing closet by type and color, 130
    rust-proof drawer units for any kind
      of storage, 246
    teaching kids the one-in, one-out
      rule, 222
    universal remote, 50
    using retractable stainless steel
      clothing line to hang clothes, 205
purge
    lotions and skin-care products, 144
    makeup, 145
    missing Tupperware parts, 75
    paper, 169, 223
    shower products, 158

R
Real Simple, 56
The Real Simple Method Checklist
    bathroom, 158–159